E-BUSINESS
To Go

INSIDER SECRETS
TO MAKE YOUR SMALL BUSINESS
A **BIG** BUSINESS ON THE INTERNET

G. LIAM THOMPSON

APPALLASO PRESS
Published by Appallaso Publishing
St. Louis, Missouri, USA

Published in St. Louis, Missouri by Appallaso Press, a division of Appallaso Publishing, P.O. Box 3985, St. Louis, Missouri 63022, 636-394-2333, www.Appallaso.com or www.AppallasoPublishing.com.

For information on licensing, foreign rights, or where to purchase Appallaso Publishing books outside North America, please contact our International Department by fax at 636-394-2216 or by e-mail to AppallasoDirector@hotmail.com.

Appallaso Press titles may be purchased for business or promotional use in special formats and quantities. For information write to: Appallaso Press, Business Markets Department, P.O. Box 3985, St. Louis, MO 63022 USA, or e-mail to AppallasoEditor@hotmail.com.

This book contains information gathered from many sources and is published as a reference and not intended to be a substitute to independent verification by users. Although the author and publisher have exhaustively researched all sources to ensure the accuracy and completeness of the information contained in this book, we assume no responsibility for errors, inaccuracies, omissions or any other inconsistency herein. Any slights against people or organizations are unintentional.

Cover Design: David Arnold
Senior Editor: Lisa Adrian

First Printing: 2001
ISBN: 0-9701517-0-5
Librarary of Congress Card Number: 00-110783

10 9 8 7 6 5 4 3 2

TABLE OF CONTENTS

SECTION II: THE PATHWAYS

ACKNOWLEDGMENTS

This book is more than a recent undertaking. It's the result of years of learning through numerous people in E-Business, and scores of others whose help and counsel predated the Internet.

First, I'd like to thank my cousins, Chuck and Janice Misfeldt, who not only introduced my parents to the restaurant business in general and to the early Wendy's phenomenon, but who have to this day always made sure I had a place in Scottsdale I could call "home." The core of much of this book is due in large part to their amazing business acumen, and their lifetime investment in me and the entire Thompson family. Numerous people have been instrumental in helping me on this journey beyond the borders of E-Business, including Paul and Karan Fleming, Jack and Anna Hayford, John and Doreen Amstutz, Jeff and Patsy Perry, Mike and Jan Andrus, Gene and Chris Moniz, Chris and Elizabeth Koerner, Oliver and Jean Lemmie, John and Ruby Darnall, and Kent and Janet Norell.

Special thanks to my partners, co-workers, clients, and friends, including the best business partners anyone could have, David and Alice Goldstein, plus Cathy and David Teson, Paul and Gretel Haglin, David "Hudson" and Jane Arnold, Mark Gust, Emilio and Sue Tellini, Rich and Merle Linkemer, LaRita Heet, Roger Yount, Chip Schafer, Sandy Coons, Drew Fitzgerald, Kevin Monahan, Steve Puckett, Lynn Beckemeier, Phil Brumbaugh, Stan Bower, Eric Peabody, Paul Scotti, Terry Ferrin, Dennis Martenz, Brian Molitor, Dan Mallon, John and Ellen Eufinger, Danny Mallon, Peg Booth, Hope Brittain-Smythe, and all of the talented editors and staff at Appallaso Publishing Group.

Finally, thanks to the four most important women in my life. To my wife, Lisa, who not only does so much every day to make it easy for me to live and write in general, but who also specifically put hundreds of hours into this book: "IWLYF." To my daughter, Tali, who makes me so proud of her convictions, and who gives beautiful words: "You're!" To my sister Carla, who taught me the meaning of fearlessness, and who personally led me to the truth. And to my second Mom, Kathy, who loves me like a son, and models so beautifully the art of resting and trusting. Thanks to all for the treasure of your support and encouragement for things in the past, and for ideas already on deck for the future. D.V.

ABOUT THE TITLE

Tired of hearing about everybody else's Internet success stories? Wish you would have jumped into E-Business years ago, or done more online by now? For those of us who have known all along that the economies and competitive advantages afforded by the Internet are not the exclusive domain of big business, E-Business To Go has a simple message. It's *your* turn now. And it has nothing to do with spending a lot of money.

There has never been a *better* time for you to open the throttle and accellerate into the E-marketplace. If you've been thinking the Internet boom was over, and that the opportunity to compete and win in the global, connected economy has already passed you by, get ready to be liberated. Everything before was just a foreshadow of what's coming. There have been only a few other times in history when so much opportunity and so many resources have combined to make so much potential available to so many people. The westward expansion into California in the 19th century that gave settlers land for almost nothing was one of those times. The G.I. Bill that opened the best colleges and universities to the soldiers returning from World War II and gave them four years of free education comes to mind. SBA loans and jump-starts for women and minorities in the 1980's was another key period. Yet these all pale in comparison to the unabridged, unfettered, global business opportunity that the borderless Connected Economy and fast, affordable E-Business tools bring to any business or organization with a computer and an Internet connection.

This is how individual entrepreneurs, small businesses, and organizations from coast to coast are radically transforming their companies for amazing, invigorated returns. This is how regular businesses with offices in places like South Dakota and Nebraska are suddenly doubling their revenues by the week, marketing to the world. And this is how you, regardless of former limitations and constraints, budget or size, can explode into the Connected Marketplace, and make your small business into a BIG business on the Internet. It's all about making your business "*to go.*"

So what do we mean by "E-Business To Go"? First and foremost, the phrase "To Go" underscores the running fast food theme in the principles that follow, as illustrated by Wendy's Hamburgers. While a large variety of products and services birthed in the USA, from dry cleaners to dog groomers and beyond, all offer services in the "to go" package format, none has done it more than, or as well as, Dave Thomas. Hopefully, when you think of "to go" and E-Business, you'll remember some of the principles herein based on that construct.

Second, the "To Go" suffix is intended to reflect some of the many new time and effort efficiencies available to the average Internet user—efficiencies that for the first time since the birth of the Connected Economy, equip us with the ability to create, launch, and manage our E-Business endeavors incredibly quickly, for amazingly low costs. The principles that appear in the front half of the book, and the many ASP site builders that are reviewed in the back, reflect these new economies of time and cost. Today, businesses and organizations of every size and budget can now enter the Connected Economy and compete head-to-head with the big boys, using E-Business enterprises that are as good as, or better than, the early-adopting 800-pound gorillas, but that cost a fraction of what it cost them to get there.

Third, "To Go" is used to signify the truly portable, virtual business that is made available today by these same principles and developments. The idea of owning and operating a 24-hour online business that literally runs itself from our homes, our cars, or our briefcases, with no requisite need for officing, furniture, overhead, or even staff, is no longer a vision relegated to the future-speak sections of Popular Science magazine. Thanks to third generation E-Commerce systems, pay-as-you-go merchant accounts and server packages, and the instant-app world of the new site-building and store building ASPs (reviewed in the last Chapters), any of us with a laptop and a phone line can be in E-Business the same day we envision it.

That's not to say it's intuitive, naturally obvious, or as easy as coming up with a site idea or URL. Adding a dot-com to the end of your company name makes you no more a viable E-Business than adding "lite" after the word Twinkie makes the Hostess snack a health food. But there *are* a number of low-cost, high-profit principles you can adopt, and some little-known insider secrets you can embrace that will give you the ability not only to compete in the Connected Marketplace, but also to win. This book is designed to get those insights and secrets into your hands, head, and heart so your E-Business will be ready...*to go.*

PREFACE

One hundred years from now, historians will summarize the Connected Era in which we are living today using adjectives and superlatives not yet invented, and make conclusions that have not yet been concluded. Like those before them who condensed the Industrial Revolution into a single paragraph about Carnegie, steel, and rails, these yet-conceived, future scholars will undoubtedly be asked to do the same about our revolution. Writing in what likely will amount to thin air, using virtual pens and invisible documents that are at once both edited, translated, and transmitted instantaneously, these 22nd century archivists will package our story into a tight, succinct summary.

Arguably, the highlight reel they produce will feature some of the "early pioneers" of our time—people like Jeff Bezos, Paul Allen, Bill Gates, and Michael Dell—who like Henry Ford and J.P. Morgan before them, dramatically and unalterably changed how the world did business, related, and lived. Yet lost in those abridged commentaries that skim through history decades at a time will be the stories of countless ordinary business owners, managers, and leaders, who did equally extraordinary things applying and integrating the Connected Age into their own organizations, with equally remarkable results. These are people like you and me, who didn't study at the Palo Alto Research Center, learn HTML programming, or get $35 million in venture capital for a dot-com IPO.

If historians confine their research to the more vocal

Internet publications of our day, they will likely conclude the pathway to E-Business success was through the inexhaustible pursuit of technology, and that those of us who embraced the Connected Age successfully, did so by becoming experts at technology. They couldn't be more misinformed. If they can get past the sensational and dig just beneath the surface of our history, they'll discover what I did: that the technology behind our digital revolution is only part of the story.

Without patronizing or minimizing the movement of electrons behind every Internet connection, I've found the real secret to E-Business success is applying good old American values and business principles *to* the technology and *through* the technology. You don't need to know how to program Flash or write Visual Basic to do it. You don't even need to hire a slew of technology experts and consultants. In my experience, if you are successfully managing an organization today, you probably already have 90% of the skills required to successfully manage an E-Business endeavor.

You just need to realize it.

This book is designed to help you do just that—and to liberate you from the notion that you need to invest in all the "specialists" and "consultants" who know the secret lingo and have the secret handshake. This book is partly my story, to simply say, "If I can do it, you can, too."

I was not a programmer, a webmaster, or even a web designer. I didn't know a single line of HTML code. And I'll admit, like everyone else, I was intimidated at first by the programmer's future-speak and the fact that I didn't know the difference between a metatag and an IP address, or that a cookie was not always a snack. When we started in 1992, there were no courses to take or textbooks to read on "E-Business for the average Joe." Yet, over time, because I was desperate, I found that there was a resource of experience that I could draw on that was as successful in its time as the Internet is today. Even though it was some two decades old, there was a business model I could use to lead my company into active and ongoing E-Business enterprises. Someone had developed a business system I could use that required neither big investments of capital nor big contracts with overpaid consultants for us to achieve success in the Connected Economy.

Doing business on the Internet is essentially about connecting people with the customized, individualized products and services they want, and doing it fast—when, where, and how they want it. When I finally saw this in the macro view, I knew I had the resources I needed. I had seen this formula before.

It started in Columbus, Ohio, when Gerald Ford was still President.

INTRODUCTION

It was 1975...long before Al Gore "invented the Internet." It was a time when "Apple" was best known as a British music publisher, when the term "network" referred to three broadcasting companies, and when "wired" meant caffeine-fueled energy. It was a period when "cable" was an overseas dispatch, when learning typesetting was a wise career move, and when starting an independent travel agency was the road to riches.

In 1975, if you wanted a hamburger, you went to McDonald's, and you got one model. It was a skinny, well done piece of meat, with a spoonful of catsup, a drop of mustard, 2-3 dill pickle slices, and some tiny little onion slivers. Oh sure, you could theoretically ask them to make your burger without the onions, or altogether plain, but that meant the dreaded "special order" yelled to the mysterious back room, and a minimum ten-minute wait. (It took a while for frozen meat patties to cook, you know.)

For many younger readers plugged into the Connected Economy today, the concept of multiplied choices and customized products delivered instantaneously to your computer monitor display, or directly to your door, is the norm. For those of us who grew up in a pre-connected world, however, scarcity, exclusivity, and demography usually meant we bought a mass-merchandised product that happened to be in stock that day. As ludicrous as it may sound to people like my daughter, Tali, who was born in 1983, it wasn't so long ago that the only jeans you could buy in the world were made by Levi's, the only place you could find them was in one select department store per community, and the likelihood of that store having any size 29-33s in stock was remote.

The idea that shopping for products or services depended on variables such as time, space, location, selection, and often luck, is a non-consideration to those born after 1980. For those of us who lived through the sixties, however, phrases like, "No shoes, no shirt, no service," and "It only comes one way," were commonplace.

There was, however, a new idea germinating in the heartland of America that would change forever the way average Americans perceived their choices as consumers. It was a radical concept that flew in the face of conventional wisdom, abjectly ignoring almost every business principle its leading competitor had used to capture the most marketshare in the industry. It was an idea that rocketed the company to become the darling of Wall Street. It was so profoundly different a concept for the time that most first-time customers couldn't believe it was possible...until they saw and tasted it.

The inventor of this revolutionary concept was Dave Thomas. The company was Wendy's. And the founding principle was customized, individual burgers made to order —hot, fresh, fast, and delivered in thirty seconds or less.

What Dave Thomas did to the fast-food industry in 1975 was as remarkable as what Henry Ford had done to the transportation industry decades earlier. By giving customers the ability to choose their own way—whether it had to do with roads or hamburgers—and by adding speed and quality to the mix, these two innovators found more than enough customers to buy, and buy again.

There were at least a dozen principles that Dave Thomas used to build Wendy's into so formidable a competitor that McDonald's ultimately retooled their own systems to mimic Dave's. These axioms are still in operation, and valid in many of the world's most popular fast-food restaurants. Without a doubt, they are among the top reasons Wendy's rings up over \$7 billion in system-wide sales and has more than 5500 stores in operation.[1]

While no one would suggest that Dave Thomas had wider audiences in mind when he first developed these axioms decades ago, to relegate them only to a history lesson on fast-food would be shortsighted. Once you get past the context of french fries, chili, and Frosties, and see that regardless of the product, the focus on customer choice, custom products, and lightening-fast delivery is the heartbeat of the fast-food business and today's successful E-business, you'll be on track for big payback in the connected environment.

E-Business To Go is about those principles, why they worked then, and why they are still working now in the new fast-food medium—the Internet.

This book is divided into two sections. Section I, The Principles, jumps right into the meat of the matter and details in Chapters 1-11 the best Internet principles and secrets to success that you can use now to make your E-Business online enterprises look and feel like some of the Internet's biggest online winners. Each chapter includes snapshots of real-world applications of the principle in focus, tools you can use in your own E-Business to help adopt and apply that principle, and a Power Test for those who want to measure their own site with regard to the particular principle discussed.

Section II, The Pathways, includes candid summaries of the top five traditional outside resources to which most organizations consider turning when they need E-Business development help, as well as what to look for—and look *out* for—when selecting a vendor or subcontractor. This section also includes a chapter on the ASP-based E-Business builders, their explosion on the landscape, and the reasons for their popularity with so many organizations today.

The book concludes with comprehensive reviews of some of the most popular of these "apps on tap" or "biz-wiz" site and store builders, including ratings on pricing, features, design options, and more. By the time you get to the end, you should not only be liberated from any constraints you may have felt competing in the Connected Marketplace, but you should also be motivated to do so with the confidence that there is nothing you can't do online as good as, or better than, the big boys.

1

LIMIT YOUR MENU

One of the first things Wendy's established was a limited menu concept—offering only that which they could do well, and deliver fast. Not offering a fish or rib sandwich actually helped, rather than hindered, Wendy's growth. As you read this chapter, think about what areas of your products or services you can serve best online, which will differentiate you from the Internet sites that try to offer everything to everyone, yet satisfy no one.

The Director of Marketing was as animated as the scene she was describing. Having come to the gathering fresh from the latest Gallery Tour at the Macromedia site, which featured some of the most amazing samples of the hottest programmers and designers in the industry pushing the envelope, she was not content to describe what she saw with words alone. Like Leonard Bernstein with a West Side Story score, her hands moved in counter rotation while her head nodded to each of us seated around the conference table waiting for our part.

If this had been a meeting where design, technology, or delivery was the agenda, I might have been more interested, and tooted my horn when cued, but because the president of the company was there on a tight schedule, and because we had to get to more important issues regarding their customers and content, I just sat there. Partly because I knew how genuinely exciting it is to discover new things online, and partly because she was new to the client's company, I let her go on. But the more she repeated words like "fantastic" and "incredible," the more I found myself not so much listening to her, as watching her. It was as if somehow the sound of her voice was turned off, and my job was to figure out the riddle of the mime being acted before me.

"And then this fairy, like Tinkerbell," she said, "flies across the screen, and our logo comes up at the same time, you know, like Apple did in the 1984 Macintosh commercial, and her little Tinkerbell wand lights up like a star, and you hear 'ding!' You know, the 'Tinkerbell ding?' And that's before you click on anything!"

It wasn't until I heard her say "Tinkerbell" in three consecutive sentences, that I finally checked back in, and decided I'd better get us back on track.

"So what are you going to do with all the extra server space and time this gives you?" I asked her. The president smiled, but the director of marketing looked at me quizzically. After a second or two she finally said, "What do you mean, 'extra?'"

"Well, research shows that for your target audience, customers, prospects, and pretty much everyone else in your industry, you have about 2.5 seconds to grab and hold your visitor with a reason for them to stay on your site. That means information, now, or I bail. The way I figure it, your little opening show will take about 15 seconds minimum for the average user to load, and another 45 seconds just to get to Tinkerbell. Which means that no one gets to Tinkerbell. They're long gone. And you've got an E-Business site behind it that never gets visited. And that means lots of unused servers."

"Oh," She said, at last dropping her imaginary wand. "Thanks. I needed that. Guess I got a little carried away."

"No problem," I said, "I think some of what you suggested can be looked at during the design and technology phase. But that's later."

With that the president smiled, and we got back to more important issues.

It's inevitable.

Your E-Business team will be meeting to discuss content issues and one of the members will want to bring up a new bit of "sizzle" he saw on a recording studio's site the night before.

"So it opens with this Hitchcock-like point of view," your co-worker might say, "where you are not just *seeing* the guitar string, you actually *are* the guitar string, vibrating sort of, and as you are plucked these eighth notes fly in and turn into cicadas that just sort of pulse there. All the while there's this zoom sound that's shushing in and out, like John Kay's riffs, you know? And you realize, those june bugs are asking me to click their wings!"

E-Business is Exciting by Nature

Sounds ridiculous, doesn't it? But I've been in more meetings than I can count where someone in the group insists on going down this "let's impress them with technology" trail. Make no mistake. Left to its own capricious course, I'd have to say that every Internet discussion I've ever been in would end up here. I'll admit— I also find it irresistible. Because the Internet has penetrated our lives so effectively, you can't help but want to talk about the latest discovery you made online the night before.

Years ago, when you first felt the thrill of being able to track your Amazon.com package in real time as it was shipped across the country, didn't you tell everyone at work? "Fifteen minutes after I saw on my screen that it was in St. Louis, the Fed Ex guy was standing in front of me with my Amazon.com order!"

The problem with allowing most of those soliloquies to get out of the gate at all is that, except for a very few industries, entertaining your Internet customers with your technology is not remotely why they came to your site in the first place. Numerous studies confirm that the top reasons for visiting and returning to an Internet venue are relevant, current, immediate information.[1] For years one of the most visited, most popular sites in the entire Internet universe was Yahoo! Finance. Its name and URL have changed a few times. Its content evolves and improves. But no matter how tempting the latest streaming, flashing, animating, moving technology may be, Yahoo! has resisted taking even a small bite of the applet. As this is being written, the site still has only one graphic, tiny 6-point text links, and every color you want as long as they're blue and black.

What Do Your Customers Want?

Wouldn't it be cooler, you say, if there was a movie at the front end? For you, maybe, but not for the majority of the Yahoo! Finance customers, who rely on this site everyday to answer one key compound sentence: "How are my investments doing today, and where can I make more money before the market closes today?"

To these users, each animation, audio clip, or extra graphic is just some other useless accoutrement that keeps them waiting longer for the information they want. Yahoo! learned this early on. Know your customers and know what they want. If your stock is tanking and you are trying desperately to see the latest quote, the last thing you want to do is wait for some dissolve effect to finish.

Consistency Is Key

When one of the world's largest chemical companies asked us to help them with their public website presentation, I didn't quite know what to expect. The new VP put in charge of their Internet marketing had described some of the frustrations customers from around the world were voicing about their online experience. It wasn't until I logged on to their site as a user that I began to understand why.

I went online and registered as a fictitious biologist from France. As a global distributor of over 100,000 chemical products, the company did a good job welcoming and greeting international visitors in their native language. The site worked quickly, was laid out beautifully, and though I didn't speak French, it looked like the text and images communicated effectively. After registering, I backed out and logged on again. That's when I noticed the problem.

Again, the site greeted me in French. Great start. But for

some inexplicable reason, the site design and layout had changed completely. It hardly even looked like the same company. Clunky pixilated red headlines in oversize pointsizes and text-heavy layouts were everywhere. All of a sudden, I felt like this company really didn't understand us French biologists. As opposed to my first experience, where the presentation communicated excellence, this time it communicated aloofness, making me feel like I was second-best. Given much more time on that site, I'm sure I would have concluded that neither I nor my fellow French biologists would ever do business with those pompous Americans again, and that the only good thing that had ever come across the waters was Jerry Lewis.

I told the company about the inconsistencies right away and together we addressed the problem. It turned out that their main site was serving certain pages from their "old" site, using the antiquated design. Although it only showed up in certain situations, this global leader realized the seriousness of the mistake and rectified it quickly with some new art and graphics.

Underwhelming Experiences

Don't try to do too much. A limited menu that delivers consistently with excellence will always outpace the unlimited one with spotty performance. If there is a single, quintessential way to guarantee that you will underwhelm, confuse, and disappoint your Internet users, it is to give them an assortment of presentations or a varying level of service on repeat visits. The Internet marketplace is not only the most flexible—allowing you to go anywhere with your message without fences or borders—it is also, as a result, the most cluttered. Positioning your Internet site and image in the customer's mind is difficult

6 Leading Indicators You May Be Trying To Do Too Much Online

1. When showing your site to customers, you hear yourself say over and over, "That section is here somewhere...I just gotta find it."
2. Your staff keeps asking for a current site map... on paper.
3. A customer calls asking why your site takes so long to load, and could you just fax her the information.
4. Whenever you walk through your networked sales order department, everyone quickly shoves what looks like your old print catalog under their shirts.
5. You ask your site manager how many total pages are on your site currently, and she gives you a range, with the caveat, "Plus or minus fifty."
6. You notice your leading salesperson's business cards, and where the site URL used to be, there is now a little yellow smiley face completely covering the address saying, "Call me."

enough to do without making it confusing yourself. Differentiating your site from the competition is tough enough without bringing more competition into the mix.

McDonald's' Ray Kroc is the grand-daddy of the consistency message and the genius behind the idea that no matter where you went for a Big Mac, you'd get the same quality, service, and price. Wendy's took the McDonald's axiom, and made it an inviolate.

It's Not About Hot Technology

Don't make the mistake of thinking your E-business system has to have the latest technology or most dramatic presentation to score with your audience. Some of the most popular sites year after year are those that have little, if any, graphics, animation, or flash. What matters is that you consistently serve that which your audience expects. Wendy's customers came to expect the freshest, juiciest custom hamburger in a paper wrapper. As long as that's what was served they were happy. Yahoo! Finance customers go to that site because it gives them immediate investing information, not because it shows a movie.

Dave Thomas had an unusually prescient sense of this when he developed the limited menu, unlimited variety concept of his first Wendy's, which continues to this day. It starts with an understanding of the customer. "People come to fast-food restaurants because they want good food, fast," he'd say. Sounds elementary doesn't it? But in the early 1970's, in a futile attempt to be all things to all people, the existing fast-food franchises had forgotten about the fast part. Burger King was promoting "having it your way," but didn't mention that it would take 15 minutes to cook it your way. McDonald's was adding so many menu items that the usual time to just "ring" the average order was a full minute. Contrast this with Dave's 30-seconds or less delivery. How did he do it?

When you limit the number of things you are trying to do for the customer, you improve your ability to satisfy the customer. "We'll never serve a McRib sandwich," Dave used to say. He knew that his system was perfectly set up for grilling the best, fresh, custom hamburgers in the world, fast. He also knew that ribs take ovens, baking time, cutting, and so much more. Was there a portion of the market that liked ribs? Without a doubt there was, but Dave determined his customers liked speed more than they liked an unlimited menu.

Different Product—Same Concept

There's a famous rib place in Kansas City called Bryant's. It's been serving ribs and fries on paper plates for over five decades. You can wait twenty minutes or more for your order on busy days. You sit on the same vinyl covered chairs that Harry Truman did when he visited, and you pay a lot more than you do for a McRib sandwich. But you get the largest pile of ribs and fries that is possible to hold on a single plate; so high you need a hand on top to keep the tower from falling over. If you believe the old hippie adage, "Never eat anything bigger than your head," then you shouldn't go to Bryant's. If, however, you want to eat the best ribs in the world, and give your body enough fuel for a week, this is your place.

The Bryant's customers don't mind waiting. They didn't come to Bryant's for fast service or fast food.

Customers can have their expectations dashed on either side of the coin. Delivering a great hamburger fast to the Bryant's customer will be met with just as much incredulity as delivering great ribs slow to the Wendy's customer.

Every year, numerous new-economy publications list top E-business sites based on various criteria. Whether industrial or service-based, whether small business or large, ultimately the evaluators weighed the major portion of their rankings on everything *except* the latest display of sizzling technology. Take a look at their lists, and you'll see what I mean. ZDNet.com, netB2B.com, theStandard.com, and Business2.com are just a few of the places you can see them.

Research year after year supports the theme.[2] In E-business, the story is always the same: "Give me what's relevant to me. Fast. Immediately. Now."[3] Dave Thomas knew he could deliver the best fresh hamburger in the industry fast, and that's what he focused on. Even though customers requested McRibs (in response to a huge media campaign by McDonald's), Dave was uninterested. He only wanted to deliver what he knew he could deliver fast, and with the highest quality.

Team members and co-workers will come and suggest things on your site that they think would be fantastic. Some may be valid, but most will not. Resist the temptation. Don't expand your menu unless you know you can deliver.

POWER TESTS FOR YOUR E-BUSINESS

HOW'S YOUR MENU?

1. Go to your site stat reports and sort for:
    - the most popular pages visited in a period
    - the least popular pages visited in a period

Compare pages in most and least categories and evaluate whether or not those in the latter group need to be on your site at all. If they do, what can you change in positioning, architecture, or navigation to increase visits and viewing?

2. Do a rough Pareto curve test. Use stats to compare the following:
    - the most popular pages visited in a period
    - the time spent on each page

If 80% or more of your site visitors spend most of their time on 20% or less of your total site pages, calculate what the cost is of maintaining the unpopular 80% of your site that serves only 20% of your users.

Could those users and those portions of your site be connected in a different way that would serve them better and faster, while improving your site? Would it be unthinkable to move them, and those pages, to something as pedantic as a paper-based system? Do you have to offer those pages or that content online at all?

2

KEEP THE NUMBERS
IN FOCUS

No other enterprise within your organization will have as much visibility, ongoing commentary, and exposure as your E-Business system. Remember that E-Business is still business, and technology and tools should support all of your business goals. When Dave Thomas was selling franchises, he always let the numbers speak for themselves.

Nothing developed before in your organization has even remotely garnered the attention your E-Business modules get on a daily basis. When you produced your last print brochure, the senior executive may have looked at it a few times, and may even have made some recommendations for the next printing run, but she didn't look at it every day. Or open it up at home every night. Or have it on display in the lobby and on every worker's desk, so that just by walking to her office she'd be reminded of it every ten steps.

Board members and stakeholders may be vocal during the tradeshow about what they would prefer to see in the booth next year, or how they think you did with the rotograph display and rear-projected video. Such feedback lasts at most a couple of weeks, and soon they're off on other more current issues that attract their attention. It's human nature. Like deer to headlights and squirrels to aluminum foil, we tend to look at things that are shiny. And nothing anyone in your organization does will ever twinkle as brightly or sparkle as long as your Internet endeavors will.

Likewise, no other endeavor will provide you with as much opportunity to shape the direction of your company in the future, and to so effectively influence even the most senior management, both now and into the next decade. It all depends on how you handle it, and them.

Being an E-vangelist

Remember, for the majority of people you work with, both in and out of your organization, most have spent the large part of their working life doing just fine without the advantages of connectivity. Eventually, that will change. Either they will get on board, or the problem will solve itself, actuarially. Until that time, one of your jobs will be E-vangelist,[1] justifying and proving why the next level of connected staff, or the next I-module expansion is advantageous or necessary. That means you have to follow the money-trail, justifying it with the numbers.

As mentioned in the previous chapter, one of the temptations that comes by reason of having a multimedia-rich medium like the Internet in focus, is that we tend to lean on the multimedia as justification for what we want to do. Let's face it. We really do have an advantage over most of the other departments or enterprises in the organization. There's nothing more thrilling than firing up a projector in a conference room and showing an Internet animation or movie that really "pops" like a Hollywood trailer. In the old days, that was about all it took for us to get an approval to do what we wanted. (We called those occasions a "Mr. Ed demo" because they were just thrilled that we could make it talk.) No more. After the demise of all the debt-ridden, earnings-lacking dot-com IPOs in early 2000, and all the

---

5 Questions To Ask To Help Keep The Numbers In Focus

1. How will we measure success or failure with this E-Idea?
2. How will this suggested plan impact our top three measurable goals now and next period, as a company, division, or group?
3. What stats and figures can we get about others who have done this idea?
4. Who wants to crunch some numbers and provide us with printouts of best case and worst case scenarios with this idea, and what it will do to the numbers we care most about?
5. If this were a new business venture, and you were trying to get funding for this, what spreadsheets would you show to get the money? What percentage of equity would you be willing to give up for that money?

"fantastic" Internet concepts that were long on sizzle but short on substance have faded, our horse today has to be able to pull weight, plow, and deliver the crops first. If it talks, too, that's a bonus.

Sizzle and Substance

There's nothing inherently wrong with wanting to make your E-Business site an audio and visual treat to the user. Advertisers have known for a century that sizzle sells, but that should not be what we rely on to justify our projects, and it should never be the sole motivation.

When Dave Thomas was looking for franchisees to buy into his new concept in the mid-seventies, he knew it was the numbers that would win the day. Sure, the product was outstanding, and the concept of custom burgers made fresh for each customer was unique. There was no question he had the sizzle, (literally), but Dave didn't make that his focus. When potential franchisees came to Ohio for the obligatory "tour" of the first stores that never failed to impress, they not only tasted the sizzle, they also took a look at the numbers. Proformas showing each of those first Wendy's stores' revenues, food costs, labor and margin were open for all to see, and see they did.

Regardless of your background, whether you were a seasoned restaurateur, or a first-time entrepreneur, when your eye scrolled down to the bottom of the ledgers and you realized margins were in the 20-30% range, you were hooked. Once you calculated that this little 30' x 76' building was doing over a million dollars a year in sales, and there was as much as a 30% margin possible on that million, the arguments were over. The numbers were what motivated my cousin, Chuck, my Dad, and scores of other seasoned restaurant veterans to put everything they had into Wendy's franchises.

One of your jobs in today's Connected Economy is to help your key stakeholders and decision makers keep your numbers in focus. No matter how scintillating the technology, or how compelling the sizzle, these will fade if your numbers aren't solid. Conversely, no matter how adamantly opposed someone is to your E-endeavor or

Internet proposition, the numbers will make your case and win the day.

A Tough Crowd

The task of keeping the numbers in focus was given to me at a client's office one day, minutes before an annual planning meeting with all the top brass was scheduled to begin. To say it was a tough crowd would be an understatement.

At least it was a crowd. Eighteen months earlier, when Raul[2], the Director of Marketing, called the first executive meeting to discuss their E-Business strategy, there had been only three of us in the room. Today, they were wheeling extra chairs in from offices down the hall. A lot had happened in eighteen months, not the least of which was that the CEO of this billion dollar organization—the same man that two years earlier had said they would never be interested in the Internet—had discovered online trading. This led to his further discovery of other benefits of the Connected Economy, and then to a papal discourse a few months back that could only be described as a corporate E-piphany. Now everyone was Internet-savvy, and Raul was past having to sell anyone on the benefits of the digital world.

This morning, however, the natives were restless. Every senior manager and executive representing every department seemed to have an opinion about the latest site upgrades. The tight quarters and elevated room temperatures didn't help the stress level. Raul and his team deftly addressed the issues one by one, until they got to the new online HR/Employees-only module. One of the new vice presidents interrupted.

"You can forget that," he boomed, pushing the paperwork away from him like a bad meal. "I'm not going to allow any employee to use company time to go on the Internet. We're not paying them for that. Ben, is there a way you can lock them out?" he asked, turning to the I.S. director.

"Well, sure, technically, we can keep every workstation from having access to the Web, but why would you want to?"

"Look, you give them an inch, they'll take a mile," the vice president said. "How do you know they'll use this HR thing at all? How do you know they won't just be surfing all day, downloading music, chatting, or God knows what."

"Good grief, Warren," Raul said. "How do you know they aren't using the phone, the fax, or our pencils for personal use? Taken to its logical conclusion, you'd have us installing those bathroom towel dispensers that only give you one sheet, because our employees are going to abuse the privilege of unlimited hand drying."[3]

The room fell silent. I don't know if it was because of the boldness of Raul's speech, or because everyone in the room was remembering the feeling of standing in front of a one of those towel dispensers Raul mentioned with wet hands, a tiny paper fragment, and an overwhelming desire to knock the thing off of the wall. As Raul and the rest of his marketing team all turned their attention my way, I realized that this was the appointed time for me to enter the fray. I cleared my throat and jumped in.

"How much does it cost to send everyone in the organization a memo?" I said, turning to the controller. "Five hundred copies in mail slots, what, no more than fifty bucks?"

"Probably less," the controller said.

"And Doreen," I said, turning to the HR representative, "how many man hours per month did you calculate your department was going to save just through the employee benefits portion of the HR module?"

"We tracked over 1,300 phone calls on average per month, taking an average, with follow-ups, of 42 minutes each, from employees asking us questions that could easily have been answered by their employee handbook, or their benefits materials. By putting these online, customized for the employee, we will save over 900 manhours per month in this area, or $27,000 in excess labor alone."

"Maybe," I said thoughtfully, "for over a quarter of a million in annual savings, a simple written memo put in everyone's box would be a better way to do what you're suggesting, Warren."

"What do you mean, a memo?" he asked.

"You know, you send out a one- or two-sentence statement over your signature that says, I don't know, something like, 'Internet access is one of the many tools and services we provide to help you do your job better. Please do not abuse the privilege, and...'"

Raul finished the sentence for me "'...confine personal use to after hours or when on breaks.'"

"Yeah, something like that," I said.

That's exactly what they did.

Numbers Win The Day

Three months later I asked Doreen, the Assistant HR Director, whether or not the system was truly saving them money, and if people were abusing their Internet privileges as had been discussed at that meeting.

"As far as using the Internet on personal time, I have no idea, and frankly, I don't think anyone even cares."

"Why is that?" I asked. "It felt like a pretty key point at the meeting."

"Not anymore," she said matter-of-factly. "Probably has something to do with the money factor. I can tell you categorically that our online HR module will account for over $250,000 in savings this first year alone. Minimum. That tends to get everyone's mind off of the occasional individual who sneaks a peak at his stock portfolio during the day, you know what I mean?"

I had to acknowledge that I did.

No matter where you are in your E-Business development, or how prosaic you think your concept is, keep the numbers in focus and readily available to anyone on your team. They can keep the recalcitrant enthused, the resistant engaged, and the ridiculous enveloped. They can be your ongoing secret weapon, silencing every argument through documented logic. You don't need to limit yourself to just one set or category, either.

A Tougher Crowd

Anne was the Director of Marketing for a local advertising specialties company that had grown to be one of the largest in the nation, partly because of their extensive line breadth, and partly because of their catalog penetration. If you needed something with your company name or logo featured, her company (which we'll call Hudson Marketing) could imprint it. It wasn't just through mugs and binders that Hudson Marketing made impressions. They also were known for their autocratic president, a big bull of a man who was the poster boy for management by intimidation, and who was convinced that the Internet was a passing fancy. This made it difficult for Anne, who early on had realized the tremendous potential for cost-savings in their print budget alone, which the digital world could bring the organization. On most occasions, she was blocked from even bringing the subject up in an executive meeting.

With her customers increasingly requesting online access to their catalogs, and her talented staff jumping ship on a weekly basis, she became convinced that the company was doomed without Internet tools. At last, she booked an appointment for us to make a presentation. To this day I still don't know for sure whose idea it was to invite all the company's managers, but if history was my guide, it was probably Mark, our master appointment setter.

When I arrived on the appointed day with my demo equipment in tow, Anne greeted me at the door and helped me set up in the conference room. Even though I was early, executives and managers began filtering in and taking their seats a full half-hour before start time. By the time I had tested the projector and adjusted the parallax, the room was almost full.

Anne turned to me and whispered, "He's here. Go ahead and start." Without delay, I lit up the screen with our opening collage.

The brief presentation came off pretty well, and for the next twenty minutes I moderated the discussion as the staff and managers enthusiastically caught the vision of what the Internet could do for their jobs and their organization. For some reason that still is a puzzlement to me today, I felt the urge to say, "Does anyone have any questions that I haven't answered?"

The moment I said it, I knew what was coming. From the

front row, where he had sat silently for the entire time leading up to that moment, the president took a deep breath, looked around the room, and asked the question that must have been simmering in his head for a half-hour.

"Yeah. I got a question," he snarled, doing one of the best Wilford Brimley impersonations I'd ever seen. "Why in hell am I paying two dozen of my people to sit hear and listen to this? What the hell is going on?"

Even though the room took a collective breath, and most of the pairs of eyes shifted to Anne, I just stood there and held his gaze for a second or two, and asked him the only thing I could think to ask.

"What do you mean?" I asked.

"I mean," he said loudly, "we're a trinket company. We sell through catalogs. Been doin' it that way for 25 years. Why in hell should I be interested in this Internet crap?"

Instantly I realized my mistake. At Anne's request, I had been focusing on "the sizzle," not knowing that the boss was still trying to find "the value." I took a breath, nodded, and quickly thought of some of the statistics I had researched.

"Oh," I said, smiling. "I hear you. Maybe you shouldn't. But your competitor, Keystone Specialties, reported they saved over $300,000 in printing costs alone last year, being online. If you don't want to save money, then I guess you shouldn't be interested. Research shows that over a third of your customers are online today. If you don't want to give them an opportunity to buy online, you shouldn't be interested."

"I should mention that your competitors who are online are stealing some of your best customers with faster orders and lower prices, but hey, they haven't been in business for 25 years like you. Your own association, the Ad Specialties Council, said in their annual meeting that members with Internet access report increasing new business by over 23%, most of it from outside their region. So you're right. If you're not interested in growing new business, saving money, or holding on to the marketshare you have now, you're right, you shouldn't listen to any of this crap. I'm sorry to have taken up your time."

With that, I turned, ostensibly to pack up the projector

and laptop, but really because I didn't want to make this a debate. Thankfully, he didn't respond, and when I turned around again, he was gone. The rest was sort of a blur. The staff filed out with their heads low. Anne apologized. I packed up my equipment. Then, just as I was about to exit the front door of the lobby, a messenger stopped me.

"He'd like to see you, if you have just a minute. Do you mind stopping by his office?"

"Sure," I said, forcing a smile. "I'd love to." Less than a minute later I found myself standing in front of a desk full of imprinted mugs and frisbees and ashtrays, listening to this same man tell me that I had made some good points, that he was sorry about the confrontational tone, and that he'd like me to come back and meet with him personally with a list of recommendations to get his company into "this Internet thing."

You Define The Parameters

There are probably as many permutations of digits and ways to focus on the numbers as there are industries. While Dave Thomas drove everyone to the bottom line, your focus may be on an entirely different calculation. I've seen clients whose focus was on the number of new customers gained through an Internet enterprise, and some whose focus was on the number of existing clients that didn't leave for a competitor. Others, like Doreen, use the numbers to show costs saved, while still others are focused on revenues per employee increased as a result of the E-venture.

In later chapters, we'll look in more detail at how keeping the numbers in focus plays out in other real world applications. This principle holds up whether it's a fast-food concept or an E-Business concept. The person with the numbers that justify his or her position will always win out over those with just an opinion. Keep the numbers in focus, even when there is good sizzle, and you'll have a viable enterprise regardless of the change in technology.

POWER TESTS FOR YOUR E-BUSINESS

HOW WELL ARE YOUR NUMBERS IN FOCUS?

1. At a team meeting, without pre-announcing the question, go around the room and ask each team member:
    - How do you feel our E-Business is doing?
    - What would you say we needed to improve, and why?

Compare answers and underscore all those that were subjective, immeasurable, or vague, and ask how they could be reworded to include measurable goals and company goals.

2. Look at all team member job descriptions and remuneration packages. Identify how many of the numbers and quantifiable goals set for E-Business appear in their documents.

- Can every task that relates to your E-Business be quantified, assigned to the appropriate individual, and measured?
- Can every element of your yearly plan that relates to E-Business be quantified with set measurable goals?

3

LET CUSTOMERS IN ON YOUR SECRETS

Wendy's had no secret sauces or back grills that were out of the customer's sight. By letting Wendy's customers see every operation, they learned the operation and made the ordering process even faster. Today's connected customers are looking for the same philosophy at your site, and those E-Businesses that open some of their secrets can gain long-term, loyal stake-holders.

Almost everything Wendy's does is in full view of the customer, and all the ingredients that go into the product are openly described, and visible. When you walk up to the front counter of any Wendy's store, regardless of the location, you'll not only see the ingredients listed on menus, you'll also see them all in open view where the expediter is building your burger. There is no secret sauce on a Wendy's hamburger and no mysterious back room from which your meal appears pre-wrapped. The fresh, sliced tomatoes, crisp lettuce, mayonnaise, pickles, and all the rest are on display, as the expediter customizes your "single cheese with everything, no onions" ten seconds after you order it.

When the Wendy's concept first appeared on the horizon in the early 1970's, scores of fast-food competitors converged on Columbus, Ohio every week to spy out this new phenomenon they had read about in *Restaurant News*. Many came with the intention of trying to figure out the secret recipes and proprietary systems that explained Dave's success. When they got to a store and began poking around, they were universally amazed. Not only was the entire operation completely "out there" for all to see, store managers would gladly show anyone how the burgers were made. More often than not, Dave Thomas himself would be at those first locations, taking orders, making his recommendations, and describing ingredients.

"It's 100% fresh ground beef, and salt, that's all," Dave would say. "We don't add any MSG, or soy protein. Now, it's in the shape of a square because, if you are a hamburger lover like me, you want more meat than bun. You decide how you want it made, tell that nice girl at the register, and in 30 seconds, you can see your sandwich made right here."

Wendy's success secrets and processes were not only made public and promoted from the first day, they were given to every customer to use and modify for their own personal satisfaction.

Seeing Is Believing And Buying

Dave Thomas figured out one of the main pillars in the success of the Connected Economy decades before the Internet was popular. Open viewing of the Wendy's procedures turned its customers into participants and sped up the ordering process. Your E-Business enterprises can probably benefit from the same openness with some of your secrets.

Michael Dell applied the "no secrets" principal to the phenomenal success of Dell Computers, where today, you can spec your own custom PC or E-Business hardware system and tool online, launch the order, and virtually watch it being built and delivered to your door. Not only does this effectively reduce the company's costs by over 10% (less labor, less paper, and fewer pre-sale conversations), customers consistently rank the self-service system as the best in the industry. Dell says that there really are no secrets in the computer business. "Everyone knows what's inside. Our success has always been 10% inspiration, and 90% implementation."[1] Customers buy Dell because how Dell does business is as important to them as what Dell sells.

Not too many years ago, when information about products and services was difficult for customers to find, and product differentiation was largely built on proprietary features designed into the item itself, it was often advantageous for organizations to keep their secrets.[2] The Internet has changed all that by bringing buyers unlimited access to sellers regardless of time, pedigree, or geography. If you are willing to open up some of your formerly classified material, customer relations may increase to your advantage as a result.

A Time And Money Saving Idea

Rubbermaid's Little Tikes Division realized just how much it was costing them to maintain some of their secrets and they were ready to make a change. Their playland equipment at restaurants and child care facilities is popular with parents and kids because of the level of quality and safety built in to every slide and jungle gym they build, but the sales process was killing sales. I first heard about it when the sales manager of their Commercial Division described his dilemma to David, my partner and our company's chief smart guy, during break time at a seminar I was giving.

"We have four people in sales support who spend 100% of their time getting proposals and bids back to the customers and reps in the field," the sales manager said. "It's a huge task, because it involves our engineering staff drawing the proposed design, then there's specs, and ultimately after about two weeks, a bound proposal with cost estimates is in the customer's hands.

8 Easy Ways To Let Your Customers In On Your Secrets

1. Send "advances" on news items, PR, and press releases one day before posting or sending publicly.
2. Ask customers their opinion about anything you are doing through instant or gated surveys.
3. Gate a "Customers only" section and give some level of privileges.
4. Open all or part of your quoting, ordering, or proposal process through an online configurator.
5. Give customers private access to select staffers' or executives' e-mail addresses or lists.
6. Create a variety of user groups, Beta test groups, focus groups, and advisory committees, and host their respective online functions and communities.
7. Post a weekly online letter or message from a manager or executive that shares not only successes, but also potential challenges or problems, and how you are going to deal with them.
8. Install a web-cam in a strategic place and give customer's 24 hour access.

But it never ends there. The customer always wants to change something, and then the process is repeated, sometimes three or four more times. Our costs to close a sale are incredibly high, and the amount of time it takes to get there is ridiculous."

What were Little Tikes' options? They couldn't ask the customer to stop making changes because there were so many variables that affected each purchase. They couldn't stop showing the customer proposed drawings of their systems, because research showed that the buyer had to see the concept before signing the order, and the Little Tikes' sales support staff was working at the fastest level of productivity ever.

"Is there any reason why your prospects couldn't see all your product options and prices, and essentially design their own systems?" David asked.

"Well, we've never given out our pricing before," the sales manager replied.

"But really, after you give a prospective customer three or four proposals, with three or four variations showing changes in costs for each one, isn't it pretty obvious what your pricing is?" David said. "I mean, isn't that what the customer is getting at, how much can I get for this amount of investment?"

"Yes. That's exactly what's happening," he said, warming to where he knew the conversation was going. "So you're suggesting we put that out there online, and let the customer figure out what he wants by looking at the pricing."

"Yes. But instead of thinking of it as just an online price list, what if we gave him some pull down menus that asked him questions like, 'What square footage do you have to work with?' 'What equipment do you know you want?' "Does it need to be ADA approved,' and so on, and then show him his options? We could have a drawing come up instantaneously, and the price for the package he just configured immediately available. What do you think?"

"I think I'm going to be able to finally reduce the costs of our sales process, and make my customers a lot happier."

Not too long after that meeting, that's exactly what

happened when we designed and built the Little Tikes' online Sales Configurator. The results were impressive. Instead of taking an average of two weeks for the proposal and quote process, customers were now seeing their project and the associated costs in real time, without delays and with an infinite number of versions to try and price. Using simple pull-down menus, they could add or delete swings, slides, and a host of other components to build their system online, and see how it affected pricing and dimensions. Instead of having salespeople going back to the customer over and over with each new proposal variation, they were now consistently closing business on the first or second visit.

I've helped a number of clients since then use the power of the Configurator to improve customer relationships through the unlocking of secrets. The online listing engine for posting medical practice opportunities that we built for Cejka and Company, North America's leading physician placement organization, is a form of configurator. Today any physician or medical specialist can see just about everything there is to know about a position or opportunity, completely online at the Cejka public site. What for decades had been information shared only in writing, and only individually, today is searchable data reviewed hundreds of times by doctors and specialists around the world through a browser.

When BASF was faced with increased competition for one of its leading agricultural brands, they turned to the concept of a Configurator as the main tool to maintain their dominant brand position. In mid-2000, one of BASF's leading products faced a serious challenge when an upstart company appeared on the horizon offering steep discounts for a generic version of the product. Though not exactly like the BASF branded product formula, it was close enough to present problems in the marketplace. BASF asked us to build an E-Business system exclusively to address this issue, and in early 2001, that Configurator launched to equip their customers with all the tools they needed to conclude that they shouldn't switch to the competition.

An Irreversible Trend

You may not feel comfortable putting all your product components and pricing online like we did for Little Tikes, but keep this in mind. Today's Internet-dependent customers are configuring their own orders and pricing their own packages everyday for other applications, both business and personal. If you have print brochures and price schedules in the field already, is it really all that secret? If the competition does go online and figure out your product components and pricing, is that really the issue? There's nothing about a Dell computer that the competition can't find online, and there's no component that Dell purchases that the competition can't purchase. Dell's secret is in the implementation, not the ingredients.

Like Dave Thomas figured out decades ago, it's not what you put on a Wendy's hamburger that makes it so popular, it's how you put it on. If you can use the Internet to let your customers in on some of your secrets, especially when it comes to product options and configurations, they'll learn more about you, and very possibly order more, faster.

POWER TESTS FOR YOUR E-BUSINESS

HOW SECRETIVE ARE YOU?

1. Scribe a critical path schematic for your organization that identifies all the places along the exchange relationship where information must pass to and from your staff and customers to realize a transaction, order, or event. Under each of those places, ask:
   • Is this open to our staff and customers? If not, what would keep us from letting them see it?
   • Is this available for viewing or collecting online? If not, should it be?

2. As an exercise, play the role of provocateur, and ask your team what is the worst thing that could happen if you posted the following on your site:
   • Your inventory
   • Your price list
   • Your job vacancies
   • Your customer complaints

4

FAST OR NOT AT ALL

Getting a hamburger order in 30 seconds was hard to imagine before Dave did it. Now it's expected. There are numerous ingredients and lots of components that combine to make a successful E-Business, but none as critical as speed. It's seminal to your E-Business growth and, like the famous 30-second order at Wendy's, is now part of the culture.

You might have thought that this chapter would be the opener, considering the ease with which I could segue from the title, and the importance of the principle. While there is no mandated hierarchy in the chapter order per se (that is, you can apply the principle in Chapter 10 without having first applied the previous nine principles), this is one principle you can't ignore. With it, all of the other elements work better, and all of your users' experiences will be richer. Service speed was one of the main reasons Wendy's took off like it did, and it's worth a step back in history to see why.

If you really wanted to see speed at Wendy's, you watched the drive-thru window. It was at one of the Wendy's stores near the home office in Ohio that I experienced a drive-thru that really *drove through*. I had purposely arrived at the noon hour to check out what was described to me as the mother of all lunch rushes in this company-run store, and at manager Teno Holland's suggestion, I took my observer's post behind the window.

You might not have any recollection of drive-thru service

pre-Wendy's, but the concept had been tried in various iterations years before, and there were a few fast-food companies in the early 1970's that were still trying to make it work. Robert Peterson was probably the guy who is known for the first multi-unit drive-thru concept, when he installed a smiling clown named Jack who greeted customers through a two-way speaker stuck in his plastic head. That grew into what is known as Jack in the Box today, and in the '70's, it was the best drive-thru in the industry.

Waiting Was The Norm

But you didn't get in the drive-thru line at Jack in the Box thinking it was going to be quick. It had nothing to do with employee's lack of hustle or commitment to service. The problem was that once you finished telling "Jack" what you wanted, your order was put on the "wheel," in line behind other orders that may be coming in from the front counter and from the cars ahead of you. So you waited for your order to get to the grill. Then, because everything started out frozen, you had to wait five minutes or more for the tacos or burgers to thaw and cook. Then you often waited for the cashier to come up and take your money, and then start filling your drinks. To get through that line in ten minutes or less back then was really an anomaly.

During college, those of us who loved Jumbo Jacks, tacos or onion rings didn't mind the wait. We were still young enough to think that spending time in our cars was therapeutic, and we really didn't have anything to do anyway.

Back then, waiting for our food

Telltale Signs Your Site Is Too Slow

1. You hear one of your staff say to a customer, "Why don't you get a cup of coffee while that boots up, then call me back."
2. You see a memo sent by your sales manager that starts, "Fun things to say to customers while waiting for pages to load."
3. You start seeing little hourglasses appearing in your dreams.
4. Your HR department asks you if you thought it was unusual that 18 of your staffers all filed for disability under the heading "nervous tic."
5. After asking your teenage son to time how long it takes your site's homepage to load at home, you come back later to find your watch embedded in the keyboard, the wireless mouse in your aquarium, and a note taped to the monitor that says, "This computer sucks!"

was the norm. I can remember as a kid, growing up in my dad's first Village Inn Pizza Parlor, thinking nothing of the fact that it took a half an hour or more to get my pizza. Sure, there was validity to the wait. Signs everywhere informed patrons to "Please allow twenty minutes cooking time for your Village Inn Pizza," as they were being made from scratch. Even when it got busy and orders were stacked up, it was not uncommon to see families waiting an hour or more to hear their number called over the intercom, "Pizza for number 327, please." Because none of us knew any other way, we accepted it. Of course, as I later discovered as a teenager, a lot of that "acceptance" mindset was cushioned by the pitchers of beer that flowed like bucket brigades to hungry, patient customers who were spending two hours or more in the building.

The time-constrained, two-job, "I'm late to soccer practice" families of the '70's changed all that, and Dave Thomas was one of the first to recognize it. That's why the franchise tours usually started and finished behind the counter of a flagship store, where Dave would allow his amazed visitors to simply stand there and watch his grand design in action.

The Incredible 30-Second Order

"Our customers have come to expect 30 seconds or less at the window," Teno said, proudly. "A while back we had a promotion where we said '30 seconds or less, or it's free.'" He let the anticipation build for a moment. "We didn't have to give away much," he said, grinning. I could see why.

I saw cars pulling into the line from the street and never really come to a stop. I watched the window as bags of burgers, drinks, and change were handed out with a wave, with the next driver pulling in right behind, money in hand. Like an Olympic relay, or a Bobby Rahal pit crew, hands exchanged money and bags in a continuous stream of movement. I heard orders over the loudspeaker and saw the custom burgers being made and wrapped and bagged before the ticket was on the cue. Sure enough, by the sweep of the second hand on the clock above the register, cars were moving through in 28 seconds or less.

In one bold move, Dave Thomas forever changed the face of the food business, and customer service expectations. There is no longer even a category for a fast-food restaurant that builds a twenty-minute wait into their process. Once you taste speed, you never go back.

Herein lies the heart of the issue for us today. If we are anything as a people group, we are in a hurry. We do more at our jobs than ever before, often doing that which took two people years ago. We cram in more activity per day than ever before. Research shows that your Internet users and E-Business customers will also no longer go back to the days of waiting for anything online.[1]

Think your industry is immune to the demand for speed?[2] Here's a scene that is repeated countless times by countless former neighborhood pharmacy stalwarts.

A diabetic retiree goes online to the CVS.com website, and asks for an extension on a prescription for a long vacation trip coming up. While online, the customer sees an announcement about Rezulin being withdrawn, and reads what other diabetics are turning to for replacement. She clicks on "refill," requests extra quantities for her extended travels, and closes the window. In less than three minutes, she logs out, confident that her vacation will not be hampered by her medical needs.

On the other end, using its extensive patient database to monitor medical histories of each patient, CVS.com contacts the customer's doctor, gets the script upgraded, fills the prescription including the extra quantity, puts it in the mail, and posts a confirmation of the order on an encrypted module on the website, with a personal note to the customer. Total effort by the customer? Three minutes, sitting in her favorite chair.

Compare that to the old way. For over a dozen years, the retiree had been visiting her neighborhood pharmacy in person, recognized by no one, often forced to stand in a slow moving line near the suppository section for the so called privilege of getting a refill. If she needed extra quantities for a trip, it meant waiting in a vinyl padded chair for half an hour or more, while they tracked down the doctor, or worse, told her to come back.

Waiting Is No Longer An Option

What the local pharmacy failed to realize was that today's customers won't stand for standing anymore, and that minutes of delay just won't work in the new economy. The fact is, this retiree wasn't looking only for a formulary fill; she was endeavoring to fill a broader need that included service, ease of communication, and exigency of experience.

This is a good place to mention one of the other trends that surprised the industry when it spiked up in 1999—the adoption rate of the over-55 crowd. You say, "Well, I just don't believe that many retired people are connected, or even have Internet access." Maybe early in the history of the revolution that was true, but no longer. One of the fastest growing segments using the Internet in 1999 was this pre-boomer demographic.

We were on a cruise recently to ports of Europe. Everyday we were at an even better location than the day before. You'd think that when Malaga, Alicante, Villefranche, Marseilles, and Portofino are just down the gangplank, the entire ship would be rushing to see the sights, but not on this Crystal Cruise.

Where was everyone each morning? There was one area on the main deck next to the library that was always overflowing with passengers. Crystal had set up over two dozen PCs with Internet and e-mail access. Guests could download messages from family back home, trade stock or check on business. Because it was a satellite-driven maritime connection, those grandparents and single seniors were sending files and photos across the globe faster than you could say "second-seating, please."

If your Internet modules and tools are anything, they must be fast. Research shows that online users consistently value the ability to find and retrieve relevant information fast. Numerous studies over the years have shown that the patience levels of the connected customer continues to shrink, with bail-outs from pages happening in just seconds. The well-worn phrase is true. Our online customers are only a click away from the competition.

There's a good reason that as far back as 1998, over 89% of purchasing agents were connected, and of those, over

95% used the Internet to research potential suppliers.[3] These experts at finding and procuring realized that the Internet gave them tremendous time advantages.

It's All About Time

Before Mallinckrodt was rolled up by Tyco, their Nuclear Medicine division salesforce had a problem. The ability to show and tell their product's story was getting hung up by the sheer volume and size of the documentation. As a product line regulated by the FDA, even sales materials had to be accompanied by requisite Material Safety Data Sheets, Package Insert Sheets, and the like. Combined with the company's own requirements for safety data, and the fact that people weren't that keen on actually seeing and touching radioactive products, the live sales pitch was seriously handicapped.

When customers turned to the Web in an effort to speed their journey to the products, they were equally as frustrated. Because Mallinckrodt had posted the print-centric Quark files for each product on their Internet site, which included all the documentation for each product, customers were forced to download huge files that took minutes each to finish, all for the want of a simple picture of the product, with price and delivery.

When Dennis, the Director of Sales Support, showed me the situation, even he couldn't wait for his little demo to download, and bailed after about five minutes!

"Why do you have to show these things in Quark?" I asked.

"Because that's all we've got. And the MSD sheets and all by law have to be with the rest of the marketing materials."

"How do you define 'with?'" I said.

"Well, until now, I guess I just assumed it meant they had to be attached," Dennis said. "What are you thinking?"

"I'm thinking that there probably isn't a single customer on the planet that actually reads all that extra text...that what your customers want is a shot of the product, a price, and delivery, period. By linking that which they want, to that which they don't want, which is all these extra sheets sucking down serious space, you're making sure that most don't wait around for the former. Do you have any stats on how many do?"

"Do what?" he said seriously.

"Do wait for the whole fat file to chug like a rat through a snake, and actually get to the products."

"Well, I don't think anyone does, right now," he said.

I felt my eyes widen but managed to hold back the initial thought. Instead, I simply said, "I think you've pinpointed a problem. Let's talk about the options."

A few weeks later, after shooting all new product photos, we were beta testing the new online system. (They needed new product shots anyway, and I wanted to get images with a high enough original resolution that we could bring the dpi down to speed load times.) Firing through the products as fast as his hand could point and click, Dennis saw the image and data load up in the browser at an almost instantaneous pace. There were lots of other customer-oriented tools as well, but the speed of the database was the main thing in which he was interested. By separating the MSD sheets and other required documentation from the product file, and making those endless forms and tables a clickable option from each product page, we managed to fulfill the safety mandates, while also fulfilling the customer's needs for fast product information.

The Brighton Account Executive and I sat in a conference room flanking the speaker phone, talking to the C.E.O. of a new dot-com client we had just starting doing some work for. A 100% online venture, this was one of the many companies that year that came to us with their "great Internet idea," looking for help. I had been asked to join the dialogue to give a second opinion on the current design of their homepage, but because it was already completed before I had been given the opportunity to participate, I told my collegues that unless I was asked point blank, I was not going to say a word.

I learned a long time ago when your grandma comes out of the beauty parlor with some woven, spun-candy looking nest thing on her head, that no matter how ridiculous it appears, if she just finished paying for it, it's better not to say anything. She wouldn't hear it anyway. The one time I had said something about "her Munster-lady hair-do," she had dismissed me with a chuckle, and said that it wasn't a hairdo anyway, it was a "coif." Whatever the heck that was.

It wasn't too long before the C.E.O. said what I hoped he wouldn't.

"So what do you thing of our new header?" he asked.

"Umm, well, it's some beautiful art," I replied, truthfully.

"Do you think it will load fast enough?" he said.

"Well," I said, stalling, "It depends what you mean by 'fast enough.'"

Obviously not pleased with my Clinton imitation, he pressed to the point.

"I'm asking you if, in your professional opinion, the average user will have to wait too long for this header to load."

"What is this average user's connection-speed, what is his monitor set at, and what browser is he using?" I said.

Without missing a beat the C.E.O. fired back, "Let's say he's on a 22.8 modem connection, monitor set to 800x600, using AOL."

Knowing this was not a time to sugar-coat the answer, with equal brevity I said, "These are huge files, created for high-res print purposes, loading as separate graphics, with animation. This average user will likely have to wait over a minute, just to see the top part of your header. According to all the current research, you are out of the generally accepted range of load time for your customer-base."

"I think that's too long," he said, "but will that kill us?"

"Consider it D.O.A." I replied, waiting for the next rapid fire question.

But the next question never came. After at least ten seconds of silence, in which the A.E. and I exchanged puzzled glances back forth to the speakerphone, he finally spoke again.

"O.K. Thanks, then. I think that's about all we needed to discuss."

And I was summarily dismissed from the conversation. Later that day I ran into the Account Exec and I asked her what they had decided to do about changing the header.

"Well, they heard what you said, but they were so in love

with the thing, that they decided to change their definition of their average user customer, rather than the design of the header! After you left they all concluded that their customers probably connect on DSLs and such, and that the load time issue wouldn't affect them so much."

I could hear my grandma all over again. It wasn't a hairdo. It was a coif. We decided not to do much with that company after that, and weren't surprised when less than a month later, it had gone belly up. (Oh, I mean, it had temporarily suspended operations.)

Everything you do or propose to do in your E-Business should filter through the question of speed. Every module or page that goes up should be tested on the widest range of systems, and the slowest possible connection. Every day you should put on your customer's hat, get online, and see which parts of your site are slow. Then do something to make it faster, or eliminate it altogether.[4]

Do you have an opening Flash, Shockwave or other animation? Give those that aren't as interested in your movie the option to "skip." If Sidney Pollack or Martin Scorcese arrive, they'll know how to see the whole thing. Do you have a long Flash script? Have the programmer tweak it so that some of the page or section to follow is pre-loading in the background, and always offer users the options of turning off music beds, narration, and other load-time intensive elements.

Do you have images that are too large, too high-res, or too fat? Reduce their size so that they load faster. Let customers click on the image if they have to see the jumbo version. Do you have scores of elements to load on a page? Cut down the number of things the user has to wait for by grouping small elements into sections which can load faster. Are you trying to say or do too much on a page? Less is more. Shift sections to other pages that are linked. Check out the leading industry sites, like Cisco, Dell, and Nokia, and see how little each page has, but how much the whole site offers.

Are you bucking trends and standards? Most of the leading sites have gone with small point sizes, limited or cascading menus and navigation, and optimized screen size.

Sure, you can design a car with the gas pedal coming out of the roof. But most people will waste time finding it. Follow the pack and imitate to produce faster delivery.

POWER TESTS FOR YOUR E-BUSINESS

HOW FAST ARE YOU?

1.   Chart your homepage load times using AOL, Netscape, and Microsoft Internet Explorer for:
   - A DSL or faster business type connection
   - A 56K or cable modem connection
   - A typical slower speed home connection

Repeat the test on loaded PCs and Macs, and then nominally equipped PCs and Macs. Compare your results with those top-ranked sites listed in your industry trades or in lists like those found at ZDNet, Webmetrix, or others listed in the Appendix.

2.   Have your team list the top ten general issues, products, or services of your company. Create a matrix that shows where on your site those elements are found, and then the time it takes for a first-time visitor to navigate those sections. There should be no pages or sections that score lower, faster times than these top ten.

5

KEEP CORE
OPERATIONS INTACT

Sacrificing the foundational basics of your business may strip away the very things which attract your clients to buy from you and not from the competition. Wendy's developed one of the tightest franchise agreements in the industry to help insure that every store followed Dave's original process exactly. Whether dealing with burgers, books, or banking, customers find security in knowing your historic services won't be diluted online.

There are two mistakes organizations can make today with regard to the Connected Economy: Underestimating it, with the idea that this Internet thing is a passing fancy much like the Nehru jacket or leisure suit of the late 60's, and thereby applying none of the advantages of E-Business to any areas of their organization; or, overestimating it, and deciding that everything the business did before 1998 is antiquated and must be completely retooled into the tone and timbre of the organizations featured in the edgiest sections of Wired magazine.

Both are deadly, but the latter will kill you faster.

I was invited to an annual planning meeting for one of the world's oldest and most successful architectural hardware manufacturers, with the Internet being the singular most important topic on the agenda. This was one of those good old-fashioned, fifth-generation American success stories. A 19th century founding patriarch stamped hinges and hand birthed what today is a $200 million dollar enterprise. If you didn't know the history and the fact that this was still a family-owned organization before visiting, you would get the message the moment you entered the company's lobby. The first time I walked into the corporate headquarters that literally braced one side of the Mississippi river, I stopped just inside the entranceway to absorb the rich history lesson which greeted me.

Generations of Success

Framing the entire reception area and running thirty feet from the front door to the welcome desk were oversized black and white framed portraits. From one side to the other it was the same. Silver-grey photos of family members in their corporate best suits, faces frozen in a stoic stare just to the right of the camera lens, mounted in the form and fashion of the wall of honor outside a high school gymnasium. And underneath each face was the person's name and tenure with the company. For those daughters of the royal family who had married, their maiden name (which carried the family and company name) was always included in the copy.

Some would argue that the array of photos with hollow-eyed stares did not a comfortable lobby make. If I were in the interior design business, I probably would agree. Even if I discovered nothing else about this clan or their business, however, the lobby spoke one message loudly and clearly: This family knows hinges. As sure as you were that the Tyson family knows chickens, and the Busch family knows beer, you knew it about this group and their specialty. Here's one of those rare commodities in the business arena —over a century of success in their field and they are still on top.

On this particular day, after the obligatory ride on the two hundred year old elevator that took two full minutes to go up one level, I entered the conference room and sat down with the Director of Marketing and his team to review their online catalog strategy. Although not destined for the lobby shrine, Dean was a wise marketing veteran with four decades of experience in the industry. Progress on their Internet development had been somewhat slow, but steady. Dean and his team had made strategically sound moves to take the company from the print and paper catalog era to the digital era. One of his first victories came when the family agreed with his recommendation to integrate the first online catalog with their existing sales reps' territories and field sales staff methodologies. Like most global distributors of complex products with decades of work building quality distribution channels, Dean knew that the idea of disintermediation was not for them, at least right now. So the question of changing the existing sales structure was not on the agenda.

That is, it wasn't on the agenda until one of the execs from another department popped into our meeting that morning and declared with considerable glee that he had a brainstorm about using the Internet.

A Radical Suggestion

"I don't claim to know that much about marketing, but I think I know where this company will go in the next century with the Web! Look," he said conspiratorially, "We all know that to make it in today's economy, you have to move to online direct. I've been surfing a lot lately, and just the other day it hit me. We could be the next Amazon.com! You see what I'm getting at, don't you? Forget the reps. That's wasted money. All we have to do is take orders!"

For a moment, I wasn't sure if this manager was pulling our legs or being serious. The look on Dean's face told me it was, unfortunately, the latter.

"No need to even bother with our architect advisors, field reps, or even the sales force, huh?" Dean said sardonically. "There's an idea. Let's fire everyone who personally interfaces with our customers."

"Listen, Dean. You're one of the old-timers," he said. "The Internet is the wave of the future. You'll see it my way soon." With that, as fast as he had interrupted us, he was gone again. We all just looked at one another with eyes as wide as saucers. Dean finally broke the silence with a line that was as right-on as it was hilarious.

"Having guys like that come in here and talk to us about the Internet, is like having cows come in to devein shrimp. It will never make sense," Dean said. After the laughter died down somewhat, he got us all back on course. "Make no mistake gentlemen, we may be changing the way our catalog is delivered and how our product drawings and such can be accessed, but we are not changing the way our customers do business with this company. We have over a hundred years of history and experience in this, and I can tell you categorically, people do not spec and order our products without help. That help can come from one of our sales reps, one of our architect advisors, or from one of our sales or customer service people out of this office, but there is no way we're going to cut people out of our equation."

Don't Mess With The Basic Formula

Wendy's practiced this same philosophy of keeping core operations intact, even as they pushed the envelope in pioneering new ways to serve their customers. In the midst of all the innovation that birthed the 30-second drive-thru, square-shaped burgers, fresh ingredients, and later, fresh baked buns, Dave Thomas drew the line when it came to innovations that changed the heart of the business.

A franchisee in Illinois had been crunching numbers one day and had calculated that the cost of having two grills open during the lunch rush was not insignificant. He had determined that besides the cost of the energy and extra wasted product, the labor for a second grill person added up. So he covered up the drive-thru grill, cut staff, and ran both sides of his lunch rushes from the front grill.

When a Wendy's district supervisor spot-checked the store, and saw the shrouded grill on the drive-thru side, he was stunned. After the rush was over, he huddled with the franchisee, who proceeded to show the supervisor his calculations. Sure enough, this franchisee's costs during the period went down a little, but the explanation wasn't interesting in the least to the supervisor. As the story goes, he pulled out a copy of the franchise agreement, pointed to a certain paragraph, and smiled at the creative franchisee. Within five minutes the second grill was open, hot, and loaded with burgers.

The paragraph the supervisor pointed to was supposedly the one about the authority of the franchise to "pull the shingle" of a franchisee if they don't adhere to the Wendy's formula. The last thing a franchisee wants to imagine is a 2,300-square-foot building sitting there with all references to Wendy's removed. No matter how well you could replicate it, people just won't come to a former Wendy's store now renamed Wanda's.

There was no question about this franchisee's math, just his thinking. The problem had to do with one of the core values. While this shutting down the second grill during a rush did achieve some minor reductions in the cost battle, it clearly lost the service battle. Order times had ballooned to over a minute each, while the order accuracy level tumbled. Having the front grill person running from the front line to the drive-thru line created havoc with both lines, and food costs due to mistakes skyrocketed. All of that paled in comparison to the violation of one of the core principles that set Wendy's apart. As mentioned earlier, one of the founding pillars of the Wendy's revolutionary concept was speed of service. Thirty-second orders were the rule. The only way that service can be accomplished on both lines is by having a grill person on each grill. As the supervisor was all too aware from the experiments in Columbus, Wendy's customers expect that service, so don't mess with the formula.

Great Technology Won't Mask A Bad Idea

"Pat," the new Director of Marketing for a leading healthcare manufacturer that specialized in patient support products like oxygen tents, respirators, and breathing machines, had a challenge. One of the new products that had been developed before his tenure was a portable airway sonar device that was intended to help doctors find the right pipe in a patient's throat. As anyone who has watched ER could tell you, it's very important in that tightly constricted confluence of pipes where the pathways for food and air intersect, that the intubation tools go down the trachea rather than the esophagus. Most first-year med students learn early how to look down the throat, identify the vocal chords, and slide the respirating tube down the correct lane. Years before Pat had arrived, someone in the company had decided that they could make a fortune building a device that sent sound waves down the throat, and emitted a different sound depending on whether or not it was aiming down the airway, or the digestive track.

That was the theory, anyway. Five years and big bucks later, Pat had inherited a finished working product that just couldn't be sold. In a last ditch effort to turn the thing around, Pat asked us to build a short interactive animated demo that illustrated how the product was intended to be used, with the idea that they could send it out to doctors and hospital prospects on floppy disc, as well as put it on the Web.

It took us about three weeks to complete the mini project, and as a self-contained little applet that was designed to fit on a single floppy disc uncompressed, it turned out pretty slick. We had subcontracted the anatomical graphic arts to a medical illustrator friend in Canada, who did an amazing job at creating all the cross section views of a patient's head and throat, and the product being used. We added a number of sound clips, navigation features, and roll-over hot spots that allowed the user to quickly see and hear the product in use. We even did a little animated movie clip of a submarine using sonar, to help explain the technology. As shown in the program, if it was pointed down the digestive track, the sound made a low-pitched moan. If was pointing down the correct airway path, it made a happier, higher pitched sound. Lights on the device changed accordingly, as well. We were pretty happy with the program when Pat presented it, as were many of his in-house staff, but the company's product managers were noticeably silent.

5 Low Risk Ways To Keep Your Core Operations Intact Amidst Wild Ideas

1. Set up a research team for the new E-Business model apart from your existing one, and test the concepts in your focus groups, studies, and roundtable discussions.
2. Spin off a Beta test product or service with as many caveats as possible, and offer your customers the opportunity to test it for you.
3. Create a separate and distinct online presence with a new name, logo, and team, and test the concept viability without factoring the parent company. If it flies, embrace it as yours.
4. Move to the next logical, tangential product or service, and see if you can make that work. Then go for bigger moves.
5. Test the concept in the marketing arena by sending a mailing or running an ad. Before you proceed, gauge the responses. If it's a dud, you've only lost the cost of the test.

Pat pressed them until one of the seasoned veterans spoke up. There was only one problem. In real applications in emergency rooms and hospitals across the country, no matter where in a patient's throat a doctor pointed the little device, it always emitted the low-pitched moan. What's more, as the product managers would go on to tell us, the whole idea that an E.R. worker would take the extra time before intubating to actually shove this other device in a patient's throat, and listen for a tone, was ludicrous. To them, where time was of the essence, even if the thing did work right, they wouldn't use it. In a word, the product was a bust.

"That's it, then," Pat said. "We'll pull the plug on this device, and cut our losses now."

Immediately, the sales manager, who had championed the concept from the beginning, spoke up in protest.

"But why?" he asked. "With this interactive demo, it looks great! We can sell it just from the disc and website module alone. The program is finished. The product is in stock. Why not use the technology to make some sales first, and recover our investment before we bail?"

"Because the product is D.O.A., Rich," Pat said softly. "It stinks."

"But look at this interactive demo! You can't say after seeing it illustrated like this, that it stinks."

"Yeah. You're right. It is a great presentation. But no matter how fancy you make your demo, Rich, no matter how many submarines and throat cams and flying graphics you throw on there, there is still no amount of wizardry you can conjure up that will make this product stink any less. The demo is great. The product is a fizz. The only thing we could possibly do worse than the debacle of building this thing, would be to show this demo to people and get orders for this product. G.T., thanks for your fine work. Please submit your final invoice, and then destroy the masters."

Sometimes, one of the best things you can do for your organization is to pull modules off your Internet site, because they are presenting a shinier view of reality than you can deliver.[1] The same forces that work so well in communicating your facts so powerfully and expansively online, do the same for your fiction. Make an exaggerated claim in a brochure, and it's read by a limited audience, and can always be labeled "old news" by reason of its printing date. Make that same exaggerated claim online, and it's seen by an unlimited audience, who expects it to be current and correct.

It's Not A Panacea

There have been scores of stories about companies who messed with their core formulas, elevating their Internet enterprises too high, or implementing online theories too fast, to disastrous results. Many in the late 1990's thought that by simply adding the suffix "dot-com" or the prefix "E" to their products, ideas, or titles, everything became new, and that which had worked so well before had to be scrapped for the Connected Age. Things like business plans, customers, and Accounting 101 were almost unjustly forsaken because of this false idea.

Was it good customer service when Value America employees were running to retailers like BestBuy and CompUSA to buy computers and electronics to fulfill their online customer's orders during the Christmas season of 1999? Probably. At least it was innovative. They knew that fulfillment was important, even if they were out of stock. When you find out, however, that they were buying these products for more than the selling price given to their online customers, and were losing money every time they rang up a new order, is it any wonder that 800 employees were let go at their December 29th post-Christmas party?

Here was a company that had been named the tenth fastest growing Internet company by Worth magazine. Its board of directors included titan Frederick Smith of Fed Ex, who invested $5 million of his company's money along with $5 million of his own; and Vulcan Ventures president Bill Savoy, who brought $65 million of Paul Allen's money with him. Just eight months earlier, the Value America stock was trading at over $70/share. Now it was under $2.[2]

When Whirlpool, the largest maker of home appliances in the U.S., joined with publishing giant Hearst to launch Brandwise.com in October of 1999 because of their "mutual desire to get a deeper understanding of consumer buying habits," is it surprising that the venture was shuttered in June of 2000? What possible value could Hearst bring to that equation?

When Disney jumped into the crowded online toy market in August of 1999, by purchasing Toysmart.com for what was said to be between $40-$50 million, is it any surprise that when that money was burned up in less than nine months, Disney shut it down? Likewise, Nickelodeon's entrance into E-Commerce toys, RedRocket.com, shut down unsurprisingly less than 18 months later. According to *The Standard*, "Toy executives attribute the shakeout to a range of factors, the most obvious being a lukewarm stock market that has left venture capitalists skittish about forking over more dollars to sites that shed cash faster than they take it in—a problem afflicting companies across the Internet."

My view? These companies left their core operations and strengths. Producing TV and movies does not make you an online retailer in a crowded competitive market, even if you do have some stores in malls.[3]

Should we be surprised that DrKoop.com was DOA after less than two years in the marketplace? I, for one, always appreciated the good doctor when he was in Washington, and speaking as Surgeon General. I know that he was simply the "front" for the Internet-wise younger founders, but to me, as much as I liked the man, I just never could make the connection from the grandfatherly advisor to an online entrepreneur. Maybe it was the beard, or the Sgt. Pepper uniform with all those gold stripes, but when it came to Internet business gurus, Dr. Koop was not one who came to mind.

No industry today can ignore this principle. Research shows that even banks have had to rethink their online enthusiasm. According to eMarketer's *eBanking Report*, banks came online out of fear only to discover the threats of their doom were not realized, and that only a very small percentage of banking business was actually conducted online. As it turned out, people still feel more comfortable banking in person.[4]

Start by keeping your core operations, the formula that

has worked already, intact. You can always tweak and change these individually in the future, in a well-researched process of testing and validation.

POWER TESTS FOR YOUR E-BUSINESS

HOW WELL HAVE YOU KEPT YOUR CORE OPERATIONS INTACT?

1.   Print out a copy of your organization's Mission Statement, Business Strategy or Strategic Plan Summary, and circle all the words that are foundational to your core. Write those words and phrases along the top x-axis of a matrix. Now call up your new E-Business system or plan, and write those major elements along the y-axis. Circle any that are not easily slotted under the top categories, and probe with team members the validity of that portion of the E-Business in the long term.

2.   Extrapolate and project a best case scenario with any E-Business element that departs from your core, and assign the highest possible level of success to it for a five-year period. Look at the bottom line and the resultant shape of your company and ask yourself and team members:
   • Is this what we want to be doing in three years? in five years?
   • Do the numbers and results in this hyper-favorable scenario illustrate that this is a brilliant move, or mere fantasy?

6

FIX MISTAKES UNEQUIVOCALLY

Once you resolve to let customers in on some of your secrets, and deliver your online ventures fast and consistently, the occasional mistakes and problems that inevitably come provide another opportunity for your E-Business to win customer loyalty. The culture you establish with all team members regarding errors will signal whether you are serious about this E-Business environment and deliver what you promised.

One of the most startling things I ever witnessed at Wendy's during my first store tour was the way they handled the occasional mistake.

The fact that they made so few mistakes on the hundreds of custom hamburgers per hour they served is another story. Remember in the mid-1970's, when we were all conditioned and trained by McDonald's that if you wanted anything on your hamburger besides the dill pickle slices, a glob of catsup, a drop of mustard, and those tiny onion slivers, you were going to wait. Then, with no regard for Pavlov, Dave Thomas re-engineered the way hamburgers were made, and instituted the incredibly fast system to build each person's sandwich with exactly what they wanted on it. Whether you were in the mood for the full load of mayonnaise, catsup, onion, tomatoes, mustard, and pickle, or if you wanted no condiments, or just one condiment, or all the permutations of extra anything, your fresh hamburger was built and delivered in thirty seconds.

The person on the front line who held the key to delivering all these custom orders quickly and correctly was the expediter. Standing next to the sandwich maker and grill person to her right, and with the register person calling the orders over the loudspeaker to her left, the expediter did three main things.

First and foremost, she listened and logged each order in her head, holding it there as a benchmark for thirty seconds before the next one came in. Second, she watched the grill person and sandwich maker assemble the fresh custom order, mentally checking off each one from the virtual order in her head. While doing so she would fill the drinks, chili, and other items needed to complete the order. Lastly, she would help wrap the sandwiches, place them on the customer's tray or in the "to go" bag, give each one a smile, and move to the next one.

Every once in a while, between steps two and three, a flag would go up in her mental checklist signaling that a hamburger was being made incorrectly. It could have been the fact that the customer requested "everything except mustard," and she saw mustard going on the sandwich. It could have been the fact that someone ordered a "triple cheese" and the sandwich maker was loading up a "double cheese" by mistake. Whatever the problem, no matter how seemingly minor, the expediter always did the same, mindblowing move. She would reach over to the sandwich maker's station, and while repeating the correct order for everyone to hear, she would pick up the hamburger with the mistake and drop the entire thing like a bomb into the trash can.

A Shocking Scenario

The customer, who usually at that moment was standing in front of the expediter waiting for his order, was almost always incredulous. They would tell the expediter that she could have just scraped the unwanted mustard off. They'd tell her that they wouldn't have minded the pickles this time. They'd sometimes ask if they could fish the rejected burger out of the trash! Whatever their comments, they were moot. In less than fifteen seconds, the expediter had helped the sandwich maker fix a brand-new, correct burger, and with an apology for the extra wait, had slid the now-accurate order to the customer.

When I witnessed this drama unfold the first time, I was as shocked as the customers standing at the counter with their mouths open. I think I might have even whispered to the expediter something like "Could I have that?" pointing to the trash. (I mean, with all due respect to George Costanza, it was wrapped up and I didn't mind mustard.) My thinking was fixed later that day when I returned to Wendy's headquarters, and Teno Holland explained it to me in no uncertain terms.

"Here's the deal," he said in a professorial sort of way. "A customer who gets his hamburger exactly the way he wants it will usually come back. Maybe tell a friend about us. A disappointed customer, who just paid a little more for that custom burger but we got it wrong...he'll never come back, and he'll tell dozens of his friends about it."

I nodded, but must have still had a quizzical look on my face.

"Look. If we start scraping condiments off of your sandwich, that's the mental picture you'll walk away with. We have to demonstrate to the customer that we mean what we say. If you didn't want pickles on your burger, we're not going to scrape them off, blot the vinegar off the meat, and hand it back to you! Don't you ever do that! I would rather throw away ten sandwiches, and win a customer, than save a little food cost that day. Don't forget, for most people, they are still learning about us, even here in Columbus. We have to shake them out of the golden arches way of thinking and into the Dave Thomas way of thinking.

The 7 Worst Things To Do When You Make A Mistake Online

1. Wait for the customer to inquire about rectification.
2. Limit communications to your customer about the problem by only sending e-mail, without talking in person.
3. Send an automated e-mail response with a generic greeting such as, "Dear Customer."
4. Ask the customer questions about order details that you should know, like, "When did you place the order?" or "What was your confirmation number?"
5. Allow anyone in your organization to deal with the customer.
6. Solve their problem or rectify the mistake without ALSO offering money back, a gift, or something of value FREE for their trouble.
7. Throw the customer back into the general customer pool, and don't flag them for special treatment next time.

We're trying to prove to people that we really can deliver through this new system. That means you get your order exactly the way you wanted it, no scraping allowed."

For many of us involved in the ongoing development of E-Business endeavors today, we're also trying to prove to our stakeholders and constituents that our new online system, module, or tool can really deliver what we promise. Even with all the press coverage, the buzz, and widespread use throughout the global marketplace, we still have to deliver every time, and prove it every time. It doesn't matter what we did last year. No matter how well we did launching an e-catalog, the day we start upgrading that to E-Commerce, we have another clean slate.

Don't get lured into the notion that speed is a panacea, and that your customers won't mind that you delivered the wrong thing fast. In an article in *Inc. Magazine* discussing the tendency for new online companies to value getting to market above everything else, Jim Collins writes: "In fact, being first seldom proves to be a sustainable advantage, and usually proves to be a liability."[1]

Small Glitch—Big Opportunity

When Activated Multimedia helped Rich Linkemer launch his online training system in 1997, there was no precedent for the concept in the Board of Professional Registration in his home state of Missouri. That's all changed now, but back then it seemed like every day we were in the business of proving our system was better than the other options out there. Up to that time, professionals needing Continuing Education credits had to either sit through a number of live, four-hour classes, or do a correspondence course where books and tests were sent back and forth in the mail.

By the end of 1997, we had helped Rich get the Board to approve this new kind of "distance learning," as they called it then, and officially launched the online training to professionals in the St. Louis area. Everything was going along swimmingly until one day a student used an online bookmark in a way we hadn't envisioned, and he ended up losing all of the progress he had made on the course. He sent a very gracious and explanatory e-mail to the "Technical Support" address available on the site, detailing how he had completed all the chapters and quizzes, was ready to take the final exam, but then got called away so he set a bookmark there. He then returned to the site a few days later and logged in, expecting to see his previous progress in the course bookmarked, as it should have been. For some reason, that bookmark had disappeared, and it looked like he was going to have to take the entire course over again. Needless to say, he didn't want to do that.

Fixing More Than The Technical Problem

We fixed the technical problem right away, but I was more concerned with this student, and told Rich so. On a conference call, I asked the team what we could do to make this right for the student. Some suggested mailing the guy the course on paper. Others insisted that he had to go back to the beginning, because that was the way the system worked, and just tell him we were sorry for the technical difficulty. One of the programmers who was on his way out audaciously remarked, "What does he expect with a new system, perfection?"

That one frosted me, but before I could comment, Rich jumped in.

"I'll manually go in and take the entire course for him," Rich said, "bringing him up to the place where he actually left off. I'll send him an e-mail link right to the final exam, where he should have been. I'll call him on the phone and make sure he's able to do it, AND I'll give him his money back."

"How are you going to get in to take the course without paying for it?" one of the staff said. "That may take us some time to manually load you in."

"No way," I said, "we can't make this guy wait anymore. This is our fault; we should fix it on our time, not his. Isn't there an easier way to get Rich into the course?"

"Well, you could go in as if you were a real customer, and pay for course with a credit card," someone said. "But you don't want to do that."

As if it had been scripted, both Rich and I spoke up at

the same time. "Yes we do," we said in stereo, and both pulled out our credit cards.

Less than an hour later, the student received the e-mail that Rich had promised, passed his exam, and gave Rich a good evaluation. I don't know if he ever returned to the site the following season to take his CE courses. I also don't know if this single incident where we went overboard in correcting a mistake was ever spoken of by him or us again. I do know that the philosophy of reacting and responding to mistakes like this was key in the overall acceptance of RealEstateExpress.com in the marketplace.[2]

During that first season of online training for real estate professionals, we were the only Internet-delivered training school in the entire state, and the Board of Professional Registrations was not yet fully convinced that we, or online training as a methodology, could really deliver. While it is not uncommon for traditional, live-training schools to get a few complaints each year from students filed with the Board for a variety of reasons, as long as they are not gross violations or significant in number, it wasn't a big deal. Because we were literally the test-case for online training in the state that year, we determined that we had to have the best track record of any school.

We didn't have a flawless execution that year. As a matter of fact, we had loads of problems with the servers and the secure payment issues, but by establishing the fact that we would fix any and all mistakes with an overwhelming response (usually giving students their courses entirely free), we ended the year with only one recorded complaint filed with the state.

That first season, we did everything we could to prove that our Internet system was a good deal, and had a valid and valuable proposition. We ended the year with around 1,000 courses sold. The following season, that number jumped to over 3,000. Many would say that this was due to the super value proposition that our online learning provided. I feel strongly that the increase was equally due to our attitude toward fixing mistakes. Take a look at your philosophy and posture toward online mistakes. An aggressive, proactive approach will pay back big dividends in the long run.

POWER TESTS FOR YOUR E-BUSINESS

HOW WELL DO YOU FIX MISTAKES?

1. Ask a friend to contact your site's customer service or help desk by e-mail, phone, and letter, and describe a fictitious problem. Ask the friend to give you a brief summary of how your team did with regard to:
   • Speed of response
   • Personalized attention
   • Process resolution
   • Demonstrative attitude to win the customer back
   • Post resolution follow-up by manager or supervisor

Add any other categories appropriate to your organization and share the results with your team.

2. Have a staff member analyze your site as a first-time visitor, and list every occasion where a promise or commitment is made. This can be as oblique as saying you'll send a catalog to anyone who requests it, to promising that a salesperson will call them within one business day.

Test each one more than once over a period of time, and identify any place where the promise was not kept at all, or within the allotted time period. Bring the results to your team or the people responsible for fulfilling these promises, and scribe an immediate corrective action.

7

SHOW MORE THAN TELL

There are dozens of ways to communicate on the Internet, with text playing an important role. To forget about the power of pictures and other multimedia tools in the face of increasingly impatient site visitors is a recipe for failure. Sometimes one simple image can say more than a whole module of text.

Before Wendy's burst upon the fast-food landscape in the early 1970's, the one thing you never found in your "to go" bag of hamburgers was a one-inch stack of napkins. Usually you didn't get a napkin at all. Why? Think about it. Did the hamburger they served at the golden arches ever drip juice or condiments while you ate it? Of course not. Those burgers you may recall, had been made long before you walked up to the counter and placed your order. They started out frozen months before in some packing plant in another state, were shipped to the freezer of the franchise you had entered, and eventually had the life and bejuices cooked out of them by somebody you couldn't see behind the racks. Then they had been topped with dill pickle slices, one glob of catsup, a drop of mustard, and the requisite onion slivers, and wrapped in a paper to sit under a heatlamp until you finally asked for it.

Most people today know the Wendy's story, and the focus on fresh meat, cooked to order, with juices and condiments in such healthy amounts that even the most careful customer will have drippage. The hot-n-juicy message wasn't always popular. In order to help customers understand the Wendy's difference and drive the message home, Dave Thomas stumbled into an amazingly brilliant marketing tactic. It would cost each of his stores a little bit more in paper cost, but it would communicate something to every customer in a way that even some TV advertising couldn't.

"You automatically get extra napkins in every bag," he'd say proudly, grinning at the thick stacks.

In no time, it was part of the Wendy's operating procedure and was the heart of some of the most successful advertising the company did in that decade. There were even TV spots that were solely clips of people wiping their mouths after each bite, for the full 30-second reel. The images said it all.

The E-Business enterprise that you manage should have a place for telling your story, too. While it is true that the top reasons people will come to your online enterprises is "relevant information, now," that does not mean that you reduce your online presence to what effectively amounts to a digital card deck. Once visitors discover that you do have the products or services that satisfy their needs, and that you don't waste time connecting them with those resources, they'll start noticing the other elements of your site, and try to get an impression of you as a company. That's where your story comes in—the differentiating factors that separate you from the other millions of pages added to the global network each day.[1]

Every Organization Has Something To Show

You may think that your existing image, identity, or niche in your market is a difficult story to tell. Maybe you think the story you do tell is a little dry these days. Never before has there been such an opportunity to quickly and affordably make so many major adjustments to who you are, and how you are perceived, as there is now. Dave Thomas did it with napkins, and it was pretty inexpensive. We've got it even better. Only in this medium where you don't have to reprint 50,000 catalogs or mail out the latest brochure in order to instantaneously reach your customers, can you reinvent yourself so easily and effectively. It may seem like a long time ago, but in the previous century when Jeff Bezos first launched Amazon.com, they only offered books. He was quoted as saying they would "never get into other products." He later changed it a little and said they would only be into books and CDs. Today, Amazon.com has so many categories of products that they've run out of room for tabs at the top of their site. Only in the Connected Age can you reinvent yourself so easily, so many times.

The sin of omission is just as poisonous as the sin of commission, and those sites that omit graphics and images completely are the ones that consistently show up in the lowest ratings. For example, the Worst of the Web awards like the "Mud Brick Awards," annually list those sites that judges hold in the lowest esteem. In 1999, one of the worst "muddies" was the state of Texas' website. The reason? It featured only "a single muddy graphic" with the rest being text. According to Rafe Needleman, "It basically says, 'Welcome to Texas, now go away.'"[2]

The secret is saying it with images more than with words. Keep the text short, but the impression long.

You say, "Well, we don't have a simple prop like a napkin that can tell our story." That's okay. I'm not advocating Dave's example as prototypical, or even appropriate for the Internet. What I am saying is the principle holds up, perhaps even more so today due to the speed of the Internet Age. Too often we're hamstrung by marketing and communications rules and traditions that have no place in the connected environment. Think of your story as something you have to tell in three seconds. See how ineffective all that text becomes?

Changing The Face Of A Company

This was the heart of the project we took on for one of our long-term customers. Bunzl Distribution USA was in the midst of changing their image. As a $1 billion plus distributor of paper and packaging products to grocery, bakery, and deli markets worldwide, they had grown to be one of the leaders in the marketplace through their eighteen-wheel fleet that blanketed North America and Europe. In short, the company was known by its trucks, rather than its services, which was okay for the 1990's because that's what the market expected. At the close of the decade, one fact became crystal clear to Paul Scotti and Eric Peabody. They could no longer afford to be thought of as a distributor with a nice fleet of trucks. They had to be known as the company that helped stores manage their inventory more effectively.

It wasn't just a marketing pitch, either. Over the years, through creative programs with customers and innovative scheduling options, Bunzl had begun to utilize just-in-time deliveries. This helped them to effectively eliminate the store's need for extra warehouse space, and gave back to those grocers the expensive square footage that could be better used for revenues rather than storage. Paul and Eric had been leading the campaign to spread this good news to their entire market, but they were running into a frustrating hurdle. Much of the Bunzl collateral and promotional material that was already in the field still had the trucking theme and imagery plastered all over it. Like most purchasing agents, their customers never threw anything away, but, also like most other purchasing agents, their customers did use the Internet—a lot.

So guess what one of the first things was that we did to reach these guys? What took less than fifteen minutes to construct, but which was seen by over 50,000 Bunzl customers and prospects that week? You guessed it: a new homepage, without even the hint of an axle, tire, or hubcap in the frame.

In short order, we had transformed the Bunzl site. A few key images of trucks were pulled down and replaced with

6 Clues You Are Telling More Than Showing

1. The staff members who develop your site content are primarily writers.
2. The navigation tool used most is the scroll bar.
3. You do not have an image library at all.
4. You hear staffers say that customers "read the page" rather than "view the page."
5. The form designers from the IRS think your site is cutting-edge.
6. Your online site proofing team has all gone blind.

inside shots of warehouse space and paper products coming in the back door. Digitized footage of their top three warehouse videos we had shot the year before were now accessible along with the streaming video players for anybody who didn't have one. Using a global find engine, except where absolutely necessary, any verbiage remotely resembling the word truck or trucking, was excised.

Today, Bunzl Distribution has more trucks than ever before, and more distribution centers in North America than any competitor. If you asked the average customer today what business Bunzl was in, even though the trucks still pull up to the same loading dock, and have the same markings as before, most will mention paper products or warehousing.

Shocked By Text Overload

I wandered by the office of one of our site designers one afternoon and poked my head in. "Show me something new or cool, Chris," I said, as was my habit when I saw him working away feverishly. Chris was a great developer with a pretty good head for site design, who could also pour in scores of pages of content an hour and make it look easy...even before ASPs were popular.

"Not today, boss," he said with a sigh. "Working on the vending machine company."

I looked at his screen again, not sure I had heard him correctly. I had been in on one or two of the first meetings with the president and owner of this local firm. Even though it had been a while, I clearly remembered the direction the site design was going, and it wasn't anything remotely close to what I saw on Chris' screen.

"Am I looking at a tech specs page here or something?" I said, bewildered.

"You wish!" Chris said, never taking his eyes off of his work. "This is the main product page. How do you like the products?" he asked, chortling.

As he worked the guffaw into a full-bellied laugh, I looked again. There were no products on the page at all. Just section after section of text blocks, broken up only by an occasional emboldened phrase and product number.

"What happened to all the images? The diagram of the mechanisms? The application photos?" I said.

"It's sad, isn't it? This is what the client said he wanted." As quickly as he had been able to work up a laugh, Chris turned quiet, looking sad as he stared at the unbelievably crowded page. He hated to be involved with any site that was destined for failure, and this one was clearly on course for a crash landing.

"Good grief," I said. "This is nothing like the concept I heard Ray express. Put the brakes on, Chris. Don't add another line or letter of text. We have to revisit this with the client." So that's exactly what Chris did, to his delight, and that's exactly what we did, as a team, with the owner of the company.

It turned out that in an effort to spend as little as possible on his site, the client had told our team to lose the images and product diagrams on those key pages. You could, in the literal sense, say that we were doing just what the client wanted. In the larger context, however, I found out he said it to one of our project managers in response to the news that, since he did not have any decent images to start with, we would have to do some digital rendering to get them all looking sharp. Which meant a change order with some extra time and costs charges on it.

In what I could only imagine as some E-version of "chicken," when the client made the ludicrous suggestion that we include no images or graphics, (apparently hoping that we would flinch and throw the extra work in for free,) our project manager called his bluff, and said, "Okay. Whatever you say." Rather than suggesting some other options that wouldn't single-handedly torpedo his project, he crossed out the change order, and continued to his next meeting. This might have made for an interesting negotiation point, and even some high drama, but the fact that he left the room with that decision standing was wrong.

When I tracked our manager down and asked him about it, he agreed with me, and essentially said that he had always intended to talk the owner out of that decision, but sort of forgot. By this time, we had hired someone to replace that project manager, so we invited the client to meet with our entire team. In less than an hour, we got the project back on track, including images on the key pages, which we agreed to clean up and place for no charge.

The ironic thing about the situation was everyone knew long before the regrouping meeting that having too much text was deadly. Like doctors always say, the difference between a healing prescription and deadly poison is only the dosage, and in this case, the text was killing this site. Not surprisingly, David met with the team right after that and made it clear to everyone that no matter who made the request, if the client's ideas are antagonistic to sound E-Business principles, they should alert the team to an infection which needs treatment before the whole project dies.

It takes almost no time or effort to dump pages of text onto your site, and it's easy to fall into the "telling" mode. Saying it shorter, by trimming copy and staying in the "showing" mode, may actually result in your communicating better, and in your visitors remembering more.

POWER TESTS FOR YOUR E-BUSINESS

HOW WELL DO YOU SHOW MORE THAN TELL?

1. With your monitor set for the screen size your customers use, go to your most important pages online, starting with the Homepage. Excluding main navigation and headers that repeat on every page, measure the amount of "real estate" taken up by text, by images (including graphics and other non-text elements), and by "white space" respectively. (White space does not have to be the color white; it is simply space that is not filled with anything, and serves to buffer your other elements.) Calculate the ratios. If your Text:Images or Text:White Space ratios are greater than 2, ask your team:
> • Is it absolutely necessary to have this much text on this page?
> • Is there a less text-dependent way to tell this same story?
> • How can we lower our ratios? Can we add more white space or images here, and send some of this content to another page?

2. Step back from individual pages, and go to the macro view. What are the top three things you want your customers to know about your organization, no matter what, after visiting your site? With Dave's napkins in mind, ask yourself and your team:
> • What are some visual ways we can convey these key messages to our visitors that tell the story without words or text?
> • If the amount of text on our Homepage is irreducible, what pre-Homepage intro or stinger could we create, that would be less text-heavy?

8

GIVE FREE REFILLS

Much of the Internet's phenomenal growth and continued popularity can be traced to the underlying principle of giving away something for free—whether it be access, content, community, or even products and services. Promoting an environment that encourages providing certain things for free is a smart way to do E-Business and a proven pathway to long-term customer relationships.

Have you ever been halfway through your sandwich or fries, reached for a cold gulp of soda, and realized you didn't order enough drink to go with your 1/2 lb. meal? There's nothing more frustrating than having to go back in line at the counter with your empty cup, and having to wait for the line of new customers ahead of you to flow through so you can have your turn. Except, of course, if you go through that effort only to find they are going to charge you full price again. By the time you get back to your meal, if some industrious worker hasn't already cleaned your tray and half-eaten burger off the table, you end up taking a bite of cold meat anyway.

Dave Thomas changed all that when he instituted the idea of free refills. It's an inexpensive lesson for all E-Business leaders to model today.

At Wendy's, when you ran out of soda or coffee, two things were different. For one, you didn't have to go back in line behind the other new customers who were placing their initial orders. Even with the 30-second rule, as popular as

Wendy's was, standing in line still would have portended some extra delays. For refills, you simply walked up to the pick-up station, handed the expediter your cup, and she filled it up directly. No waiting. No cold food.

Second, you didn't have to pay for that instant refill, either. At Wendy's, you could get as many refills as you wanted, just for the asking, at no charge.

Early Freebies

One of the first elements recognized as a hallmark of successful Internet sites was the idea of community. Many have written about the power of giving like-minded visitors an online home where they can enter chat rooms, share resources, and build relationships. There have been more than enough experts to explain the sociological reasoning behind community, why the grouping of demographic and psychographic segments online is popular, and even why North Americans spend more time chatting than Europeans. What many miss in these reports is something much more elemental and basic—the factor that enables and equips all these millions of communities to exist so easily and propagate so rapidly to this day. It is the fact that these communities are free, and that they continue to provide free stuff to their visitors.

Not too long ago, everyone loved to talk about stickiness in this regard, with the purists elevating the value of a site's content in community to such overinflated importance that it seemed for a time that unless we hired George Will or Bill Buckley to write content for us, we were in trouble. It turned out such a notion was, in a word, hogwash. Excellence in content wasn't the seminal issue, as those who attempted to eke out a few bucks for the passkey to their communities found out. If you want to see some good definitions for unstickiness, take a look at those sites that had killer content and leading-edge community, but which also tried to charge for it.

Despite Michael Kinsey's reputation, Salon.com couldn't get people to pay for the online privilege of digitally hobnobbing with leading thinkers of the day, and reading some truly riveting work.[1] After seeing subscribers bolt for other sites that had no cost, in what was undoubtedly a solely altruistic gesture, Microsoft decided in early 1999 that their online financial site, msn.moneycentral.com would be free to all users effective immediately. The idea of charging someone for realtime stock quotes also went quickly by the way of the leisure suit.

The reason Getty Images and eyewire.com have seen such logarithmic growth in their customer base, in my view, can be traced back to their decision to buck the trend in the industry to give users free access to their libraries, free use of comp images, free design tips and tools, and free lifetime storage of any and all images selected, even if not purchased.

Giving The Razor To Sell The Blades

With all due respect for King Gillette, it's a razor blade market now, and if you want real growth of your E-Business customers, you may need to give away the razor in order to sell some blades. Research confirms it again and again— your site visitors will increase both the frequency and duration of their visits if you give them some free benefits or values that reward their patronage.[2] The good news is, in the Internet world, they'll give you information about themselves, sometimes in great detail, if you do the same. The key is to always make the request for information or attention part of an exchange that gives them the cost-free benefit in return.

This principle extends across all types and flavors of E-Business and is not limited to those that are offering products for sale. In fact, the most successful Internet sites today give "free refills" for things other than money or commerce exchange transactions. I did a short review of some of my favorite sites, and confirmed it, to wit:

"By giving us your name and areas of interest, we'll send you our free newsletter every month at no charge."

"Register now for a chance to win the free trip to Paris."

"To use the full-range of free services on our site, simply use the registration wizard below, and you'll open up the entire world of online research."

Roger C. Parker calls this open content, and says it can

include everything from articles about disease prevention (for humans or pets) to special insider deals, or reservation privileges for upcoming video or music releases.[3]

Today's connected customer has learned to expect free refills, and it's up to you to keep your site from falling into the old economy template of features and benefits. It's easy to do. There are a host of inexpensive, and in many cases free plug-ins and modules you can install on your site that will build repeat visits, including:

- Instant Surveys
- Daily News Feeds
- Customized Newsletters
- Preferences Storing
- E-mail Notifications
- Software Downloads
- Auction and Exchange Systems
- Research Information by Industry
- Instant Messaging
- Games
- Training Courses, and more.

Even though you can add most of these free things to your site relatively easily, you don't necessarily have to go outside to come up with these kinds of offerings. Take a page from almost every major hotel, airline, and car rental company today, and send personalized e-mails to your constituents offering deeply discounted or loss-leader pricing on perishable commodities in your inventory. As those in the tour and travel business have shown, an empty room or seat left unsold today is better given away for a dollar, or free, than just left in inventory. Take a look at what you have on hand that might fit into the same category. In your industry or niche, if you sent a weekly e-mail offering this inventory as a special bargain or free to your online members only, you should see some spikes in your growth.

Another Option

Another increasingly popular way to achieve the same result is to build a different site that serves as a virtual

100% free resource. Monsanto Agricultural did this when they launched their Farmsource.com site, and gave away a wealth of their research and training to farmers at no charge. If you looked closely at the bottom of the homepage, in six point type you'd find Monsanto, but everywhere else, it was just Farmsource.

When Activated Multimedia, Inc. was one of the only shops in the Midwest doing Internet development, we often spent an inordinate amount of our time explaining and evangelizing the new Connected Economy, often to the detriment of other equally important tasks. In order to keep us from killing ourselves with meetings, and to help accelerate the sales curve, we launched the E-Business Resource Center.

We designed our new concept—E-BusinessEd.com—to do two things. First, it provided an easy, user-friendly online resource of all the latest E-Business research and case studies, so that our customers could be better equipped to sell the ideas internally. Second, it hosted a free online community where other members could share their experiences and needs in an unregulated, free, and uncensored environment.

Free Things You Can Give Away

1. Downloadable anything—white papers, software, or music, etc.
2. Customer administrative services—tools and modules to make their jobs easier.
3. Connectivity with peers—chat rooms, bulletin boards, auctions, or P2P messenging.
4. Industry content you can syndicate—news headlines, weather, stock prices.
5. Training—online tests, assessments, courses, and fully-stocked libraries.
6. E-mail messaging and notifications—automated e-mails personalized by customer preferences and sent as a service.
7. Membership—to private areas, clubs, special pricing, games.

We were so convinced we could convert people into the Connected Era revolution, who would in turn do the selling for us, that we gave away seminars, tapes, and even best selling E-Business books. I'd have Cathy order a dozen or so of the top ten titles, we'd take delivery and put them on a shelf, and whenever a visitor registered, Cathy sent them a book with our sticker on the inside cover inscribed as "a gift from G.W. Thompson and the EBRC."

Some would say it was foolish to do that without promoting Activated Multimedia, but even if no business came to us by way of the EBRC, we knew there were more key people in some of St. Louis's biggest companies jumping on the E-Business bandwagon as a result. Back then, we really didn't have much in the way of competition. Word got around that if you wanted a quality Internet package that came in fast and on budget, you called Activated.

Now, of course, the competitive landscape has seen more growth, and we're not the only game in town. Everyone from the Big Five consulting firms, to the other communications firms and ad agencies who are getting around to changing their own signs, claims they do E-Business, I-Business, or M-Business in some manner or fashion...but we still give free refills.

Today, after every meeting or presentation we give, or after every phone call or inquiry that comes in, we send out a free best-selling E-Business title. That extra 12 ounces of soda cost Dave Thomas about three cents back in the mid-'70's, but the lifetime value of customers who returned for lunch day after day, week after week because of it was exponentially greater. Sending a best-seller can cost us $25. Posting new case studies or research takes time, but because I want customers who are repeat visitors, who come back more than once, I consider it a minimal investment that can pay back huge dividends.

You'll know it's working when you hear your customers mention something that you know they picked up by way of the freebie. Recently I was in a strategic planning meeting with the marketing team of a new Fortune 500 client we finally landed after about 18 months of dialogue. The conversation had shifted to the subject of search engine rankings, and how they were consistently buried when keywords were entered into the top seven engines. At one point one of the senior members muttered something about "who cares?" I was all set to jump in with some of my favorite research about the subject, when the director of marketing beat me to the punch and said: "Ladies and gentlemen, here are the two things you have to remember. Statistics show that over 90% of all purchasing agents use search engines as their primary research tool today and over 53% of all connected users specifically turn to search engines as their main tool for prepurchase information!"

Like a proud parent, I sat there beaming. He got those stats from one of the white papers I had sent him, and he quoted the two leading headers of the main section verbatim! What was the total cost for the free refills we sent out over a year and a half? It was probably less than $100. What was the value of the business we ended up getting from this client? Let's just say it was a great investment.

Give customers something free. Like Dave Thomas discovered over three decades ago, the wise E-Business manager will make it easy and obvious to customers that there is no waiting, no ringing, no paying for these free products and services that are part of their relationship with you.

POWER TESTS FOR YOUR E-BUSINESS

ARE YOU OFFERING ENOUGH FOR FREE?

1. Identify every place on your site or within your E-Business where you ask visitors or customers for something, even if it's as minimal as clicking an "I agree" button. Compare that ledger with the number of times you give them something. Ask yourself and team members:

   • Are we giving visitors more than we are taking? If not, what can we offer them at these key places that will tip the balance?

   • Are we communicating early in the visitor's experience that they will have special privileges as our customer, and will get benefits that include freebies and no waiting in line?

2. Put together an informal focus group of peers and ask them to tell you what they remember about your site's homepage that you will be showing them. Then reveal the homepage and allow them to look at it for only three seconds.

   • Do most of them mention one or more of the free items you are offering?

   • Do they remember what the free items are, and how to get them?

9

LEVERAGE YOUR INGREDIENTS

Developing content for your E-Business enterprises can often be a daunting and time-consuming task, yet approached creatively, it can provide significant ROI from other venues. Those who want to get the most mileage from their online content can learn a technique invented by Dave years ago and repurpose, repackage, and reconfigure every single element that makes up the site.

My first introduction to Wendy's chili was through my head, not my mouth. One afternoon during the time when my Dad was first checking into this new franchise, he had invited me to join him at the kitchen table, where he had opened some pro forma statements from one of Dave Thomas' representative stores in Columbus. Frankly, I was neither experienced in, nor interested in, learning what all the rows of numbers and columns meant on those mint green ledger sheets, but I did know how to find the bottom line on such statements, and I did know an amazing pre-tax profit when I saw it. As my eyes widened with amazement at the revelation, my Dad just grinned and pointed, anticipating my question.

"Here are the three secrets to Wendy's success," he said, illustrating his thesis with the ever-present ruler he loved to use as a pointer. "Revenue per square foot," he began. This was rooted in the amazing number of orders the store could process in a 2,200-square-foot building. "Relatively low labor cost," he continued. This was primarily a result of higher sales figures. "...And of course, this amazingly low food cost," he summed. He was clearly pleased with himself on this one, but the puzzled look on my face prompted him to go on.

"Look, when we were in the pizza business," he said patiently, looking more like Tom Bosley by the second, "we were known for the freshest ingredients, the highest quality cheese, sausage, pepperoni, and all, just like Wendy's is today. The difference is, when we finished the day at Village Inn, most of the ingredients that we didn't use were thrown out. We just refused to give our customers day-old ingredients, or frozen ingredients, no matter how much it hurt to trash the surplus. We tried to calculate yields, but never planned exactly right, and to be sure we never ran out of ingredients, we always had extra. That made our food costs hover in the higher ranges."

Still not sure where this was leading, and trying hard not to sound like Richie Cunningham, I tried to get him to cut to the chase. "Okay, but what does that have to do with this amazingly low food cost, for a hamburger franchise that mandates fresh meat every day, and prohibits freezing?" At that time Wendy's was the only restaurant that ordered ground beef for delivery every morning, and would "patty-up" the day's needs for that unique, individual store. (Even today, if you visited your local Wendy's in the early morning, you'd see the first shift cycling hundreds of pounds of fresh ground beef through the Hollymatic patty machine, that formed Wendy's unique square patty.)

This was in stark contrast to the way McDonald's, Jack in the Box, and the others approached it, ordering from a central commissary and taking weekly deliveries of frozen meat patties. It seemed to me that Wendy's system of fresh ground beef each day would mean a higher food cost for the same waste and yield reasons Dad had experienced with Village Inn.

"What if I told you all of the extra ground beef that each store didn't use at the end of the business day was not thrown out, but thrown into a pot, simmering on the back stove with tomatoes, onions, beans...?" His voice trailed off enough for me to finish his sentence.

"The chili!" I said, nodding. "Fantastic. The most

expensive ingredient in chili is the beef, and in one brilliant move, you get two paybacks—salvaging what would otherwise be thrown out and having a constant source for tomorrow's slowly simmering, highest quality, lowest cost chili." I glanced again at the ledger, and smiled. No wonder so many entrepreneurs were trying to get a piece of the Wendy's pie. Dave Thomas had a formula that, in 1975, anyway, was as good as it gets in the food business.

It's a formula that still has application today in your E-Business, with even greater results. The beauty of the Connected Economy is that you can leverage your digital ingredients even easier than Dave Thomas did with physical ingredients. Ground beef, no matter how well managed and used, is still finite. That is, if it's in the pot of chili on the back stove, that portion of ground beef cannot also be in a triple cheese at the front counter, or on the grill waiting for an order at the drive-thru. Your digital ingredients *can* be— because ones and zeros are infinitely replicated with no degradation of the original source. Your E-Business elements can be duplicated, ported, repurposed, reused, and repackaged effortlessly, as much as you want, as many times and places as you want, with little or no cost.

One Item—Many Wrappers

This is a trick some of the largest technology companies use all the time. If you go online and check out what Cisco, HP, Dell, or even "Big Blue" offer to their online visitors, you'll see what amounts to their best sales pitches, recast in a variety of different packages. Whether they are presented as industry white papers, research reports, handy calculators, or case studies, it's all essentially the same content tweaked a little to match the framing of each vehicle. This has become so popular a concept that these same white papers, case studies, and research reports are now showing up on portals, exchanges, and industry news sites as information resources.

You can also repackage ingredients into a more active delivery system. Marry this idea with the power of one-to-one e-mail news, and your customers can theoretically be getting every bit of your best content, just delivered in bite-sized pieces.

How does this work out in practice for those of us who are not as big as Cisco, or those of us who don't have a fraction of their staff? One summer not too long ago our little team hosted an E-Business seminar in a public venue that filled to capacity so fast, we had to add a third session to accommodate the ground swell of business leaders who wanted to attend. Like most people who speak at gatherings in an industry they love, I had more than enough energy that day to do three sessions. If you asked attendees in each of the three—as we did, formally, using critique forms at the end—you'd find that all three gave me pretty high marks. If you asked my associates, however, they would tell you I said and did things differently in each session, and that certain points were made better in the morning, afternoon, and evening sessions, respectively. They'd also tell you that my delivery at the middle session was much better than the first, after I had eaten something.

Sure enough, they were right. When I looked at the video tapes and critiqued each one I had to agree, I was a cold fish in the morning! I found myself wishing that all those who attended the morning session could have seen me in the afternoon, and heard some of the examples I had shared during that session exclusively. Then it hit me, and I realized we had a

10 Sure-Fire Ways To Leverage Your Content

1. Repackage application information into white papers that are downloadable online, sent in mail, and offered at conferences and tradeshows.
2. Repurpose individual eCatalog pages as embedded e-mails sent regularly to prospects.
3. Burn all Flash modules, site animations, and videos on self-running,self-looping CDs for lobby and tradeshow displays.
4. Use an automated translation program to send international prospects links in their own languages.
5. Hook up with industry portals and affiliates to post pages or links on their sites.
6. Videotape your speeches and presentations in the PR section of the site.
7. Convert site Glossary sections into downloadable or printed manuals.
8. Assemble weekly online surveys and opinion polls into research reports that can be sold, distributed as premiums or used for leverage to get press and PR in your industry.
9. Repurpose your best screen art and graphics into screensavers you distribute online.
10. Send a business card CD, including any online calculators or configurators with a letter to prospects and stake-holders.

way to make it happen. It was a way to serve the content in a variety of packages and wrappings over and over again, at little or no expense to us.

More Sizes And Shapes Of The Same

On Monday morning I went back to our office, and outlined my plan with the production team. David was on his way out of town for two weeks for a much needed vacation, so he gave me his blessing to superintend the production staff while he was away. As usual, I came with the ideas, leaving the programming and facilitation to our team members. "Two weeks from today," I said confidently, "with your help, I'd like to have the following completed and available to the public." Then, to each person, based on their specialty, I described what I thought could be their contribution to this idea of leveraging the content we had just presented at the seminars.

To Andy, one of our programmers, I asked if all the case studies that we shared could be made available online, with access from two different pull-down menus. One menu would list the case studies in the form of questions that start with "How can I...?" The other menu would list the case studies by subject, in the form of "Tell me about..." Both menus could lead to the same library of cases, just through different pathways. As usual, Andy said, "No problem."

To Cathy, our office manager, I asked if she could reformat the content into a new white paper, with the same case studies in print form. She said, "Sure." We decided to entitle it "The Top Ten Internet Secrets Your Competitors Hope You Never Learn."

I asked Bridgett, our online training programmer specialist, if she could convert the content to Internet-based training format, and call it something like "E-Business 101." She said what she always said: "Sure."

To our outside videographer, Larry, I requested an edited and compiled version of the same seminar, taking the best of all three sessions and editing them into one single VHS video that we could offer as another resource to our customers through our online store.

I then asked our freelance developer, William, who had the latest digitization software in town, to compress and convert that same VHS video to online streaming video format, for us to use as mini online clips.

I gave LaRita the assignment of sending PR releases to the trades, based on the case study stories from the seminar.

I asked Jason to put together an easy system to send personalized e-mails to all the attendees, with embedded HTML and links to the places on our website where they could review any of the case studies or points we made in the seminar.

I asked Marshall, our sales manager, to come up with a new churn letter or call to prospects that announces that one of these new reports or resources is now available to them, free, just for the asking. (When they did ask for something, Marshall would leverage a meeting out of it by suggesting that it was no trouble at all for him to "come by and drop it off in person.")

Not surprisingly I guess, for this staff anyway, almost to the person everything that I had outlined was done in some shape or fashion that allowed us to leverage that seminar content into over a half dozen repurposed, repackaged products. Since then, some or all of that same content has been copied and pasted into countless broadcast e-mails, quotations, proposals, articles, and subsequent new E-Business sites we've developed for ourselves or sister companies.

Research confirms that leveraging your content is also an effective way to keep the public portions of your E-Business sites fresh. If you want a guaranteed kiss of death for your site, then use stale, static content. If your visitors and users return to your online home and see the same dry meals on the table, the same half-full beverage bottles laying around the living room, the same track from the CD playing over and over again, they'll bolt. No one wants to waste their time, and serving up yesterday's leftovers sends that signal to the repeat visitor the moment they realize you have nothing fresh to serve.

Plan For Multiple Uses

There's another approach to repurposing which you can build into both future content and modules, that anticipates multi-use applications. It's essentially the preplanned recognition of the relationship between the whole module and its individual parts, much like analysis and synthesis. Put whole sections of content in one place, and then put small portions or segments in another. In the same way that publishers release a single chapter of a new title through a magazine before a book's release, you can get more mileage out of every ingredient you create for the online environment by spreading it around.

As I've mentioned before, one of the ways you can add a level of sizzle and quality to your E-Business presentation is through a Flash module. Because they are essentially a compact little animation that you can delegate to a Flash programmer[1] to produce for you as a subcontracted project, you can control the costs and keep your involvement to a minimum. Once you have that Flash module, repurposing it into other tools is easy, and a great way to leverage your investment.

I came up with this idea sort of by accident one day, but it's a neat trick that you can use with relative ease. Ed, the marketing director of one of our longtime clients, and I, were discussing the Flash tour we were putting together for him. It was designed to introduce his web customers to their online catalog and shopping cart system. Like most of the Flash modules I'd managed, this one was going to feel like a movie, where the user would see fifteen screens appear and dissolve over a continuous music bed and narration. In this case, the entire program left to run on its own lasted six minutes, and each screen had about 25 seconds worth of content.

As a tour to introduce their online catalog and commerce system, it moved along at a nice pace. Each of the fifteen screens had a number of bullet points flying in, timed to appear at the right place in the narrator's voice-over. Each also had a number of images and screen grabs that were animated to show what the mouse movement and navigation looked like when using the e-catalog.

It was when Ed started to discuss a different project, that of building an FAQ section for their Help module on another branded site, that this Flash project came up again. "You know," he said, "the content for the Flash tour is pretty good. Is there any way you could take that content from our corporate site, and put it into the Help section over here?"

"It's an idea," I said, "but most people who need help won't have the patience to wait for the thing to play. Depending on what they are looking for, it might take five of the six minutes of run time just to get to their subject."

That's when Ed asked the question that unlocked the answer. "Is there any way you could have an index of all fifteen screens' subjects, so they could know where their answer was?"

After a quick phone call to our Flash programmer, I said, "What if I told you that not only could the Help section have an index of the fifteen subjects or screens in the Flash tour, but that users could also select any individual screen from a pull-down menu, and watch just that 25-second clip individually?"

"You mean they don't have to wait for the whole thing to play, like on the Corporate site? That sounds awesome. How long would that take to do?"

"About an hour," I said. "Chris said it was so easy, he would throw it in at no charge with the Tour."

That's exactly what we did.

Take a cue from Dave Thomas. With just a slight amount of effort, you can rewrap and repurpose those ingredients that have been sitting around in just one context, and leverage them into a variety of newer, tastier packages. For most of your site visitors, they'll never realize that content has been repeated and repackaged. For the few that do, it will just reinforce your message all the more, and illustrate what a wise E-Business marketer you really are.

POWER TESTS FOR YOUR E-BUSINESS

HOW WELL ARE YOU LEVERAGING YOUR INGREDIENTS?

1. Go to your site stat reports and identify the most popular pages and content by either number of visits and/or time spent on those pages. If these elements are valid in importance, do an inventory of support tools and ask your team:
- Besides our online systems, where else do we have this content available or deliverable to our customers and prospects?
- If this content is so good or popular, should we consider repurposing it into other forms outside of the E-system?

2. Print out a schematic or flow chart of your site showing all content by name and/or category, and mark every element that has information with potential value to a customer, prospect, industry publication, or constituency. Create a chart with repurposing categories listed vertically along the y-axis, including:
- Direct Mail
- Traditional PR or Publicity Item
- Online News Release
- White Paper
- Trade Journal Article
- Tradeshow Presentation
- Monthly "Churn" Letter
- Mini-tour Module
- Online Training Course or Module
- E-mail Marketing Blasts

Add more of your own categories and fill in the matrix by assigning the content from your schematic to the repurposing categories.

10

GIVE CUSTOMERS THE ORDER PAD

One of the most powerful barriers to exiting you can erect in your E-Business system to prevent your customers from shopping vendors or jumping to a competitor is amazingly easy to do and low in cost. For very little up front investment, you can set up your key accounts with their own private personalized module on your site, and essentially give them access and power to write their own orders.

I learned how much people love to be in control of their own orders years ago, during a lunch rush at Wendy's. Until the mid-seventies, about the only type of restaurant in which you'd be able to write up your own order with the blessing of management was in a sushi bar. There was something woven into the American culture back then that categorically prevented us from thinking that self service could be beneficial. For a society that until the mid-sixties never removed the tags sewn into the underside of mattresses (under penalty of law), never pumped their own gas, and never bagged their own groceries, writing up our own orders was a stretch.

It was originally that way at Wendy's, too. Typically, when the lunch rush hit, a Wendy's worker would go out to the serpentine and take orders. Even with thirty-second order pacing, when there were fifty hungry customers arriving at the same time, lines would form. Customers would give their order on those occasions to the Wendy's person, who would mark up the order pad with appropriate notations. There was a code you had to follow that ensured the condiments for burgers were noted in the correct order, with Xs and Os the key indicators. When the customer arrived at the front register, he would hand the order to the register person, who could call it out and ring it up at the same time. The time that was often "wasted" at the front register deciphering people's orders, or waiting for them to decide, was mitigated in this way, because these things were done while they were in line.

Some of Wendy's busiest franchises altered the cosmic balance in the mid '70's by taking it a step further, and actually giving the order pad to customers in line, to write up themselves. To the amazement of everyone, once people in line got over the shock of being handed the order pad, they took to it like Catholics to a bingo card. What impressed me even more was how quickly the average customer figured out the code, and was able to write up tickets for everyone in line next to them.

There are few E-Business axioms or mandates that I think can apply to everyone universally regardless of their product or service, but this is one of them. By virtue of the penetration of some of the more popular consumer sites that recognize us by name and allow us to write up our own orders for music, clothing, vacations, and investments, the concept has become as standard and as expected as self service gasoline. Whether you think it's valid for your customers or not, whether or not you are convinced that your business is the exception to the rule, the fact is today's connected customers *expect* you to give them the order pad. They have been doing it online now so long, and through so many other online resources, that your lack thereof will stand out like a boom box in a sea of MP3 devices.[1]

You can extend them this privilege in a variety of shapes and packages, and call it different names. There are lots of variations out there. When you go to eyewire.com, for example, the stock photo images you select go to your own lightbox, which holds the slides for you until you need them, whether a day or a year from now. Sigma Chemical's dynamically driven E-Business site not only greets you in your native language, but after building the page to your specifications based on your industry and job-function, it also brings up all the chemicals you've reviewed or ordered previously. Then you can search and order more by name, composition, application, and even by atomic drawing.

Even if you don't have, or don't want to offer your customers, this level of intimacy in ordering your products or services online, you can accomplish the same effect by setting them up with an amazingly effective module on your site. It gives your customers the same feeling of power and control, but costs you very little to build or maintain. I'm talking about the customer Extranet.

A report by Spiral Media of Fortune 1,000 executives showed how important this tool can be. Of those surveyed, 29% of the executives who had developed a customer Extranet considered it "the best return on their investment" of any enterprise they had developed.[2]

The customer Extranet is one of those online phenomena that you launch, and from the very first day your customers start using it, gives immediate satisfaction to them, and immediate payback to you.[3] The principle is simple. Instead of having your repeat customers come to the site and have to start from scratch each time, as if they were a first time visitor, or a stranger, give them a gated or passcode-protected area where their order history and preferences are available. Immediately your customers can see the benefits you've provided them.

First, you've saved them time, because they don't have to fill in fields and the basic information

> **4 Natural Places Besides A Shopping Cart To Give Your Customer The Order Pad**
>
> 1. On the homepage, where they can select and set preferences for what they want to see.
> 2. Within your online catalog, by giving them options for "saving" and "remembering" favorites.
> 3. In their private Extranet, by giving them access to past order details, inventories, tracking, and so forth.
> 4. In e-mail correspondence, newsletters, and e-marketing, by giving them choices on what they want to read about.

that is so time consuming when starting a new blank order form.[4] Second, you've given them tools they can use to save money. By keeping their order history for them, in an easily accessible place, they can more readily discover buying strategies, groupings, and repeat orders that can yield savings. Third, it helps them reduce or eliminate ordering mistakes. Now there's no more transposition of SKU or part numbers and no more mistaken identities. Once the products are in their Extranet, future orders are just a matter of clicking on a box, or entering quantities.

There are similar economic and time efficiency advantages for you as well, but the real payback to your team comes from the barriers to exiting that customer Extranets provide. In short, by giving your customers all of these tools and benefits to make their jobs easier, and the ordering process smoother, they will usually not leave you for another vendor for price alone. You have their order histories, preferences, short cuts, and special pricing already in place, and that makes it hard to leave. I call it the Hertz #1 Club scenario.

If you've ever had the pleasure of seeing your name flashed above your rental car in the Hertz #1 Club lot, finding your paperwork on the seat already filled out, the keys in the ignition, and city map opened on the dash, you'll never settle for the other rental companies again. It's no contest for me. Regardless of how much lower the daily rate is from Thrifty, or National, the time it takes me to stand in line, fill out the forms (again and again), decline the insurance, and find the car, makes it too costly. Simply said, it makes for too much work. Because Hertz has effectively eliminated the requirement for me to repeat redundant information every time I need to rent, and given me time-saving benefits by doing so, they've created an almost impenetrable barrier to exiting for me. Each time I get to walk past all the other car rental stations with lines and forms and collision-damage waivers printed in small type, I am further reinforced in my decision to stick with Hertz.

Dell is probably the poster child for successful customer Extranets. Over 70% of the company's revenue comes from B2B customers, and once they are in the system, they are set up with their own online Premier Page or other appropriately named module. These exclusive customer Extranets customized for each company display only the Dell products approved for purchase, and show special corporate pricing. The idea wasn't unique to Dell. The degree of implementation, however, is. By the end of 1999,

Dell had set up over 15,000 Extranets for use by over 15,000 of North America's leading organizations. Think of it. Hundreds of thousands of computer users from over 15,000 companies go to the Dell site, log on to their private Premier Page, and simply go shopping by checking boxes. There are no time consuming forms, no internal approval hoops to jump through, and no pricing research to do. Just check, check, click. Is it any wonder Dell scores more revenues and more margins than the competition?

The system Dell has in place is sort of the Ferrari of the customer Extranet world. It's tied to manufacturing, JIT parts, and a host of other in-house systems that empower Dell to build your order from scratch, starting the instant you press "send." The customer side is just a very small portion of the bigger system. The good news is, you can affect the same result for your organization with a less detailed and less costly customer Extranet system.

We built a lean and mean version of this kind of Extranet for a tradeshow exhibit and display builder here in St. Louis. They had cultivated a number of Fortune 500 clients who were exhibiting in as many as twenty or thirty shows a year, requiring intense logistics and the coordination of thousands of booth elements. Incredibly, the display company was managing these shows and exhibits manually, with account executives and traffic managers writing every line of every order by hand. They called me in to help them with a redesign of their public Internet site because a competitor was starting to woo clients through a much better looking online presence. As soon as I saw the nightmare paperwork system in action, I shifted the focus.

"How does bioMerieux Vitek tell you what duratrans they want in the booth for New Orleans?" I said to Jon, the president. I knew something about the French-owned medical testing company's tradeshow schedule because we were doing work for them as well.

"They call us," Jon said calmly, "or fax us."

"From what I've seen of even their small island booth, you've got hundreds of elements going into one display, and that's just next week's show, right?" I asked.

"Right. We build over thirty shows for them a year," Jon

said proudly.

"What happened to the header in Chicago last month?" I asked, knowing it would surprise him. I had been to that show with the client, because we had built some touchscreen kiosks for them, and the header for the booth hadn't made it with the rest of the display components.

"Oh, you know about that, huh? Typical mistake. The customer thought they ordered it. Maybe they did, maybe they didn't, I don't know. We didn't have it on the paperwork, so we didn't ship it. It sat here in the warehouse the entire week."

This was the opening I was waiting for.

"Jon, what if I showed you something you could do to your Internet site that would give you a far better competitive advantage than just dressing it up? What if I could have a module installed that would not only help alleviate the missing header scenario, but would give you a barrier to exiting that would make it virtually impossible for your competitors to steal your clients? What if it could save you money on every show? What if..."

I was waxing it on pretty heavily when he interrupted me.

"All right, already. You've got my interest. What is this magic bullet?"

In less than three minutes, I had described and sketched out what just a few weeks later became their customer Extranet. It wasn't deep. It wasn't fancy. It didn't have half the knobs and levers that the Dell Extranets did, but it was effective. Very effective.

All we did was provide an online image database system that could inventory all the components and display ingredients that Jon had in his warehouse for customers. For his medical clients, that meant that we loaded in digital images of all the tradeshow display modules in the various configurations put together in exhibit view, and then we individually entered every duratrans, header, poster, rotograph, banner, and the like. For the average client, that could mean hundreds of separate elements for each market or tradeshow in which they would exhibit, but once they were in the customer Extranet, it was child's play. Product managers and exhibit managers simply went shopping online, and built the exhibit virtually on their private Extranet, picking and ordering the ingredients from inventory, and sending the order to Jon's team.

A few weeks after we built the system for Jon, equipping him to offer this order pad system to his key clients, he told me that one of his best medical clients, who exhibited at over twenty shows per year, had decided not to take their business to a new competitor. When it came down to it, even though they were offered a package for less money than Jon's lowest bid, they didn't want to give up the personal Extranet they had on Jon's site.

Jon thought it was because it made his company look more high tech. I thought it was more basic.

"Did everything make it to their show this time?" I asked, remembering the header problem in the previous Chicago show.

Jon said, "Oh, yeah. That, too."

There are probably as many applications for this tool as there are URLs, and Extranets can be seen in almost every industry. If you've never experienced the service through an Extranet as a customer, go to OfficeDepot.com or an online supply resource in your market, and see why this form of customer service has become so prevalent.

Set up Extranets for your customers, and you'll erect barriers to exiting, because you've made it so easy for them to order, with fewer mistakes. They'll love the special treatment and increased productivity it gives them. You'll love the fact that your competitors won't be able to buy your clients away from you on price alone.

Once your Extranet system is in place, you can then add another low-cost feature to your site that will make you almost impervious to competition. That's in the next chapter.

POWER TESTS FOR YOUR E-BUSINESS

HOW WELL DO YOU GIVE CUSTOMERS THE ORDER PAD?

1. Measure your empowerment quotient. Circle on your site schematic or outline every junction where a customer's quest for information or progress on your site is met with:
- a dead end
- a form or wizard to fill out first
- a notification that someone will contact them later
- a message that their request has been taken, but that's all
- a link to an e-mail address

Ask your team in each case what you could change to allow the customer to get the information or element right there, or continue to make progress. Compare your process to an industry leader in this regard, like Dell. Is there any reason that your site couldn't score a perfect zero in this area?

2. Run a list of your most important customers according to the criteria you consider most valid. Compare that list to your current site.
- How many of those customers have an extranet or module reserved for them?
- How many of those customers see their names or any previous order or preference information on the site?
- How difficult would it be to score a perfect 100% in this area?

11

KNOW YOUR CUSTOMERS BY NAME

Long before the Sam Malone character from television's Cheers popularized the notion that home was where "everybody knows your name," Wendy's servers were recognizing regulars by name and preferences. From now on, E-Businesses that want to grow must do the same thing.

The hot-n-juicy concept captured the hearts and minds of many in the early years, but no one in my experience considered Wendy's his home more than Tom.

Tom was a sign maker whose territory covered hundreds of miles of back road counties and burgs rarely visible on the southern Illinois map. He wasn't wealthy by any means, nor did he have a lot of free time, but no matter where his calls were on a given day, invariably, somehow, he made his way into our Wendy's for lunch. Sometimes it was at 10:30 a.m., sometimes it was after 3:00 p.m., but almost without fail, we saw Tom every day during the week.

Now I have to admit, until I saw this happen repeatedly with my own eyes, I wouldn't have believed it. The idea that a customer would go out of his way to have lunch at Wendy's everyday was off my experience chart. Sure the food was great, and the service the fastest in the industry, but to make Wendy's as much of a habit as brushing your teeth? After about two weeks of being aware of Tom peripherally, I decided to focus on him, and see if I could figure out why he kept coming back. Once I was looking for it, it jumped out at me like a bright light.

"Hi, Tom," Denise would say everyday from the register.

Tom would answer in a similar fashion, "Hey, Denise. Working hard or hardly working?" as he handed Denise some money.

As if she didn't hear him, Denise would reply over the sound of the register, "That's $2.06, Tom. Thanks. Have a great day."

With that, Tom would slide down the line where the expediter would hand him his order and say, "There ya go, Tom. Thanks."

There it was, as clear as day. Like the Good Humor man in the summer calling you by your nickname and knowing you liked the cherry crunch bar, the Wendy's staff knew Tom by name and by preference.

Everyday Tom walked up to the register and after being greeted, just started handing over his money. No order was given and there was no discussion about what he wanted. What's more, no one behind the counter seemed to ever need his order information. I would discover later after watching more, as soon as Tom's car pulled into the parking lot, the expediter would simply say, "Tom's here." Without a pause, Wendy's workers made a single cheese with everything—no onions but extra salt—filled a cup of chili, and put it on a tray with an iced tea. Denise would start ringing the order before he was through the vestibule. All that remained to be done was Tom handing Denise his $2.06, and the transaction was complete.

"Tom likes the fact that we know him," Denise would tell me later. When I asked Tom point-blank, it was as if he and Denise had read the same script.

"This is my place, ya know?" he said, crumbling another saltine into his chili. "No matter how my day goes, no matter how many rejections I get on my sales route, I always feel better when I come back here. Your people are real friendly, and I never have to tell them 'extra salt.' They remember, ya know? They remember. I like that."

You don't have to be a psychologist to acknowledge that one of man's most basic needs is to be appreciated. While Tom might be skewing the typical Maslow hierarchy a bit more than the rest of us, he does illustrate the point. Tom was hungry for more than food when he came to Wendy's, and your customers are looking for more than your product or service when they come to you or jump on your E-Business system. They seem to be saying, "Make me feel good about me, doing business with you."

Today's connected customers won't put up with yesterday's generic communications that we scribed for mass media and large demographic groups. According to a study by *The Industry Standard*, despite all the gains in customer convenience and accessibility the online environment occasions, 1999 Christmas shoppers scored online relationship issues as less than satisfactory. Fully 40% of all popular shopping sites tested by a simple e-mail inquiry did not respond at all, even after three days.[1] It was because of performance like this that the surviving consumer shopping sites invested so much during the year 2000 to be able to be better equipped for full online relationship streaming the following Christmas season.

The One-To-One Secret

Here's the way I like to put it. If you know my name, AND you know my preferences, you know I'll be back.[2] At Wendy's, Denise and the staff had to rely on memory, hand-written notes, and repetition to pull it off. Today, we've got it much easier. If there was any single activity the Connected Economy has brought to our organizations today that has supercharged our ability to serve customers better, it has to be the technology which makes truly personalized, one-to-one service an affordable reality.

If you haven't tapped into one-to-one e-communications, now is the time. As Chad Kaydo said, "It is the ultimate marketing tool. [One-to-one] e-mail is the marketing medium you've been waiting for."[3] One of the reasons for all the praise and accolades is the fact that that it is a natural fit for any organization with even a modicum of E-Business enterprises. Personalized, permission-based one-to-one communication is easy, affordable, and fast to implement for today's connected organizations.[4] As *Business 2.0* put it recently: "Permission marketing was once a niche business. Now everyone is doing it."[5]

The Connected Economy moves fast, and much of the technology and tools that are popular today will be superseded or obsoleted tomorrow by new innovations. If there was one core concept, however, that I felt would withstand the test of time regardless of delivery methodology or location, it would have to be the personalized, one-to-one e-communication. Everyone wins with this incredibly affordable tool.

Permission-based e-mail gives senders bigger returns and response rates than any other vehicle, and scores higher in perceived value by recipients. According to a study by IMT, "Permission e-mail is five times more cost-effective than direct mail and twenty times more effective than Web banners. 79% of survey respondents prefer it over opt-out e-mail."[6]

A Winning Cost-Saving Recipe

Look at this recipe. You can collect your own names, or rent lists of people who said they are not only willing, but would very much like to be sent information about your category of product, service, or industry. That'll cost you from nothing, to as much as $.30 per name. You can buy your own e-mail sending system, or rent those services, for pennies each. Unlike standard direct-mail, you don't have printing costs of $.30 or more each piece, nor do you have postage or sorting costs. The e-mail system will load in the personalized information automatically (remember, it's all about databases), but it does so at no cost for mechanical operations like printing. Unlike snail mail, there's no waiting days for delivery. Send it now and it's there now, whether you send ten or ten thousand.

Even if you rent the most expensive e-mail lists, and rent a service provider to send your one-to-one messages out, you can do so for a total of much less than $.35 each. Compare that to the average $1.00 each for a personalized letter.

It gets better still. Now crank in the best response rate you've ever had for direct mail, whether it's 1%, 2% or even 5% (you must have won an award for that one), and crunch your cost per response. Compare that to the average response rate for opt-in personalized e-mail. See how incredibly low your cost per response looks when you're getting 10% returns or more from the e-mail! (That's a conservative response rate.)[7] If you want an envelope-stretching statistic to quote on this subject at your next marketing luncheon that's guaranteed to make the rubber chicken bounce, here's one: Jane Weber, V.P. of Marketing for Promotions.com, sees response rates of up to 35%.[8] Seth Godin, the father of permission marketing, says his clients see response rates of 35%-70% for opt-in personalized marketing.[9]

Delta Airlines' e-marketing program is typical of how easy it can be and how powerful the results are. Visitors to one of their online sites invite users to specify what cities, activities, vacation types, or sports they like, and are asked if they would like to receive e-mail announcements or e-newsletters when specials in those areas come up. As in most tour and travel businesses, an empty seat on an airplane at take-off is unrecoverable for that flight, so selling that seat for half-price at the last minute (days or weeks before) can be a winning proposition for everyone.

By matching those empty seats on flights to different destinations with the preferences of their e-mail subscribers, and then sending customized specials to each one based on those preferences, Delta has been able to see increases in sales for those seats by over 500%.[10] It's easy to see why. Some of the other airlines are simply promoting routes with lowered prices, such as "Special! St. Louis to Detroit! St. Louis to Milwaukee! St. Louis to San Diego! $199!" Delta, on the other hand, takes my love of ocean sports and NFL football, and sends me only the St. Louis to San Diego pitch, putting it in the context of a "Sports Holiday."

E-Marketing With Little Expense

This isn't complex technology, either. We sent personalized e-mails to our customers in the early days of TrainingDepartment.com using a $99 small-business version of an e-marketing system for which bigger companies were paying $50,000. Except for a couple of features that we determined we didn't need, there was nothing significantly different about the $99 version!

We had a category-killing product with Training-Department.com, and the marketing was driving hundreds of new prospects to the site each month for their 30-day free trial. Once they did that, however, we were noticing a significant fall-off in activity. Customers would go for weeks without using the system, or give others the free pass to courses we had extended to them. Others were letting the thirty days expire without so much as a whimper. We knew we had to do something to get them informed about, excited about, and into, the system.

TrainingDepartment.com was a natural sell once people tried it. This ASP provided online training tools and courses to businesses for a low monthly fee. The key to getting people to try it turned out to be regular, timely personalized e-mails. Here's what we did:

When we first launched TrainingDepartment.com and began to see hundreds of training and HR managers coming to the site each week to use the system, we were thrilled. The one-to-one direct mail campaign to our core market of small- to medium-sized organizations was working better than we had expected. Most seasoned direct mail veterans will tell you that getting a 1% response-rate in today's cluttered marketing environment is a real feat, yet we were consistently averaging over 2% with our mailings.

It was almost formulaic. We would send 20,000 mailings out each month. Less than 30 days later, we would see that 400 new customers or more had come on board as a result of the mailing. Admittedly, part of the reason it worked so well and scored so much higher than other mailings was due in part to the offer. It's hard to resist a pitch that says "Try the TrainingDepartment.com system, free for 30 days," or "Let twenty-five of your co-workers take all thirty-six TrainingDepartment.com courses, free!" Equal credit has to go to the fact that we also integrated the one-to-one personalized communication style of the mailings into the online system.

Anyone Can Do An E-Centric Strategy

Here's how it worked. When I first approached Roger Yount and Donna Cooper at Brighton's one-to-one division, economy was foremost in my mind. Unlike most of the dot-com start-ups that were being written about in 1999 (before a more sober and rational approach to investing returned in year 2000), TrainingDepartment.com was not funded with venture capital, and did not have an unlimited marketing budget. If the truth be known, we were significantly underfunded in the marketing area, so I knew we had to hit a home run with whatever we decided on using to get the word out.

Donna confirmed what I had already suspected from my research; if you didn't have an opt-in e-mail address, the single most effective marketing tool you can use to get a known segment to try your product is through personalized direct mail packs. In addition to the brochure and response device, these packs needed to contain a personalized letter with interchangeable content based on who the recipient was. Our plan called for 20,000 of these stuffed letters to go out each month from Brighton's one-to-one fulfillment department. Each letter was printed individually, with a number of fields and paragraphs that included personal, unique information based on who the addressee was.

For example, if we were mailing to a titled training manager or director, the headline and copy would address training issues and needs. To the HR professional, a different set of paragraphs was used. All told, there were over 40 variations in just the one-page letter alone, which necessitated the programming of the high-speed variable field printers. To that mix we also added more permutations and combinations by changing the outside envelope, the inside letterhead design, and even the way the lists were purchased and formulated.

If we stopped there, we would probably have had a decent response simply using that level of personalization. In my mind, however, what really kicked in the afterburners and gave us the winning formula was the way we extended the one-to-one philosophy into the online environment. Instead of just asking the prospect to send back the enclosed reply card alone, we added a section in each letter that suggested that they "log on to the site now, and use this personal passcode created just for you."

The theory was, as a connected company with a totally online product, TrainingDepartment.com ought to be doing everything we can to make it easy for our prospects to go online. The personal passcode we gave them wasn't just a key to get past a gate. When they entered their code on the first welcoming page, three things happened.

Three Simple Yet Effective Steps

First, the site refreshed and the prospect was greeted by name. "Welcome, Terry, to your TrainingDepartment.com online training system." It then went on to explain some benefits, and invited "Terry" to continue. When Terry did, and came to the registration wizards, he came to the next surprise. All of the fields in the registration wizard that had information about Terry's company, address, and the like were already automatically filled in. This apparently wasn't that tricky for our programmers to pull off. They simply downloaded the databases that Brighton one-to-one had used to do the snail mailing, and poured the data into the appropriate record fields online. Since the prospect was visiting for the first time, this demonstration that we knew who he or she was, and that we were expecting them, was impressive.

We didn't stop there in recognizing each visitor individually, but let me pause to add a comment about an additional benefit that was also part of this set up. Remember we were sending out a variety of different mailings each month. In addition to all the variable fields we changed in each and every letter to make them personal and unique, we also were changing letter formats, letterhead designs, envelopes, and lists. Donna would call this "testing," and the way we tracked all these variations proved to be invaluable to us.

In what used to be called the direct mail industry, marketers could discover which lists, letter versions, and offers were the most effective by coding each one in the address field. For example, if they were testing five letter versions and two envelope versions, using three lists, the code for letter 2, envelope 1, and list 3 might be 2A3. This would show up again on the reply card. By matching each mailing code with the corresponding code on each customer's completed reply cards, they could see which letter, list, and envelope combination pulled the highest response. We applied that same system to our mailings, with a twist.

Remember the personal passcode each recipient received in their mailing from us? You guessed it. We generated these to be more than unique identifiers of the individual so that when they came online we could apply personal greetings and content. They also had the direct mail codes in them. If we stayed with the above example, the code would start with 2A3, and to that our programmers would create a suffix that was the unique identifier of the individual from the database, resulting in a code like 2A314558.

This was all done before the letters were drafted, with our programmers and Brighton's fulfillment team working together

> **4 Clear Signals You Need To Focus On Personalization**
>
> 1. After spot-checking your site from home, and filling out the registration wizards in detail, you get an automated e-mail from your company that starts out, "Dear Visitor, thanks for visiting our site."
> 2. Looking at the day's outgoing mail, you see a letter going out to G. Gordon Liddy that begins, "Dear G.," and one to Glenn Close that begins, "Dear Mr. Close."
> 3. When you ask your site developer whether cookies are a good idea for customer relationships online, she says, "That or wine."
> 4. When you ask your communications manager what he thinks of Martha Rogers, he wrinkles his nose and says, "Too prissy for me. All that napkin folding and doily dressing."

so that the personal passcodes could be included in each letter. [Note: While this still sounds incredibly difficult to me, those in database management, those in direct fulfillment, and our own developers insist that the process is effortless. They send the databases back and forth through simple e-mails with attached files, and let the programs do the rest. After the first mailing, our system at TrainingDepartment.com and the Brighton team handled the entire process in less than an hour.]

Combined with an online administration module that detailed in real time all the prospects that visited our site by personal passcode, any of the TrainingDepartment.com team could see at any time which letter version, envelope, list, and the like were pulling the most responses. It gave us astoundingly current information that translated into lightening-quick changes to the letters and much faster decision-making regarding the lists we would actually buy from month to month.

After the prospect had responded to the personal letter pack we sent, and they had come to the TrainingDepartment.com site with the personalized recognition continuing, we then put them into our personalized e-mail system. This was our automated e-mail generator that would take each of our 300-400 new prospects each month and create personalized e-mail messages every few days. Knowing that our prospects had responded to our 30-day free trial, it was incumbent upon us to encourage them to use and explore the TrainingDepartment.com system as much as possible within that month's time. I suppose if we had had the budget and manpower, we would have called each one by phone. With limitations on both fronts, the e-mail contact was our best option.

So, periodically and automatically, each prospect would receive an e-mail every few days giving them tips, tricks, and links for an enhanced TrainingDepartment.com experience. These were timed according to their first log-on, so the Day 3 e-mail was different than the Day 27 e-mail (which typically had more urgency about their 30-day free trial ending soon), and they automatically went out personalized for the user.

Many Options

I'm sure you can find companies and systems who can provide this service for you. We chose to do it ourselves with a system that cost us a grand total of $99. Admittedly, this is the "lite" version of a system that is being used by Fortune 500-level organizations who paid 500 times more for the package, but we discovered that the extra features and larger volume capability that they offered weren't necessary for our application. For less than a hundred bucks and only half a day to set up and test our system on the customer satisfaction supervisor's computer, we were in business. From then on, our CSS watched it work automatically each day, and then responded to the e-mail responses that were coming back. That was the other thing that amazed me. People were actually responding to "Mary" and "Jodi" (whose names we had inserted at the end of each system e-mail), and engaging in digital dialogues with them after receiving these e-mails.

Our strategy for TrainingDepartment.com combined the best of personal one-to-one mailings with one-to-one online recognition and personalized e-mails. The only real cost in that mix was associated with the snail mail letter packets, which on average probably cost around 50 cents each, including postage. We used the letters to arouse their interest and get them to our site, and from then on, we used the cost-free automated online one-to-one systems to keep their interest and get them to stay.

You could also choose to forego the snail mail part completely, and go with a totally e-driven strategy. This is extremely attractive if you already have your target prospect's or customer's e-mail addresses in-house. If you do decide to purchase or rent e-mail lists, you'll find they don't come cheap. While the typical qualified lists for our *snail* mailings averaged around 10 cents per name, the associated list of e-mail addresses would have cost us around 30 cents per name, and the universe would have been much smaller. On the other hand, while we were in the 2% response-rate with our letter pack mailing, and delighted to have it, well-strategized e-mail campaigns can pull an 8% response or more.[11] So if you have to buy or rent a list, run your numbers based on these different variables within your industry, and see which is the most economical and gives you the best payback. In our case, we had no choice because the penetration of e-mail addresses that was available to us at the time for our target market was less than 30%, and we wanted to reach many more. Your situation may be different.

When you look at the traditional outbound communications tools your organization uses, could you empower any of them for better results and returns through e-based communications? One thing is for certain. Whether you use personalized e-mails that are automated to fill in variable fields, or you stick with a more labor-intensive solution, the moment visitors or customers come to your site and identify themselves, you can no longer afford to ever call them by anything short of their name.

POWER TESTS FOR YOUR E-BUSINESS

DO YOU KNOW YOUR CUSTOMERS BY NAME?

1. Sort your stats to show the top pages your customers frequent, from first page visited to page exited. Identify:
   - any pages that do not have at least customer name and date personalization
   - any forms or tools that do not have customer information already filled in
   - any ancillary tools such as configurators or calculators that don't have customer information at even the most basic level

   Ask your team:
   - What is keeping us from making these areas personalized?
   - What can we do this week to fix it?

2. Look at the communications tools that are birthed from your site.
   - How many e-mails are sent out with a generic salutation?
   - How many letters, catalogs, or even invoices are not personalized?
   - How many requests for information that come from your site acknowledge that fact in the materials that are sent out?

   Gather or form your personalization team and see if you can turn the lagging areas around in less than a week.

12

USING AND MANAGING OUTSIDE VENDORS

The previous chapters have highlighted E-Business principles that can be universally applied to both existing sites and new online enterprises. For those who are in the process of E-Business development or modification, who want to explore the outsourcing options, this section can save you time and money. It starts with a look at the various consultants and outside specialists available to you. It concludes in chapter 13 with the hottest phenomenon in E-Business development —ASP instant site and store builders—which for many may be the quintessential answer to fast, affordable E-Commerce.

Your situation is unique and I can't presume to understand the complexities of your organization or your specific challenges. I don't know if you are a traditional business or organization moving to expand your E-Business activities, or if you are a new start-up geared specifically for the Connected Economy, launching what could be the next dot-com success story. I can give you some practical insight from my experiences, as one businessperson to another, and hopefully keep you from making some of the mistakes I made. I can also be a voice of reason in contradistinction to the chorus of other "experts" who will be, or who already are, insisting that you have to hire them exclusively to manage your E-Business endeavors for you. I can be the voice of encouragement against the choir of specialists who would patronize you with the implied message that since you don't know the language of their technology behind

E-Business, you can't know how to manage the business of E-Business.

Let me start by admitting again that I am not an Internet programmer. I do not know HTML, Flash, ASP, XML, Dreamcast, or the host of other coding programs that tell all of the elements on your device, be it Internet site, handheld, or wireless, where and how to load. I can't begin to tell you how a database is propagated, or how to convert HTML to WAP or WCDMA. Neither did I ever learn Photoshop or Illustrator, nor any of the other design systems available today. I never could draw a horse on paper, and I certainly can't do it on a screen.

That didn't stop me from being able to conceive of, birth, and manage scores of comprehensive E-Business systems for my own companies, small businesses, and scores of Fortune 500 and Wilshire 5000-level firms since 1995. And it shouldn't stop you, either.

If I Can Do It, You Can Do It

To help me underscore this point, let me take you back some years to Activated Multimedia's early days, and prove to you that even when you have no earthly idea what you are doing, you can have success managing these projects.

When we first started building Internet systems and E-Business solutions for clients in the early '90's, there was no body of wisdom or collection of standards to which we could turn for advice. We were one of the first multimedia companies in the U.S. that had joined the Connected Economy revolution, so often the concepts we were pitching to corporate clients were things we believed in but had never tried to build before.

The formula back then was as simple as it was ridiculous. Mark (the Bulldog) would convince some Fortune 500 executive that if he didn't want to be left behind in the new digital age, that he should meet with me. The trick (if you can call it that), in getting these senior execs to agree, was in Mark's promise.

"Mr. Thompson will be bringing a little 15-minute egg timer, and I guarantee when the last grain of sand falls through the end, he will be finished and packing up."

The reason I didn't ever feel like it was a trick was that I really did have a little timer that I borrowed from one of my daughter's board games, and I really did have the ability to be in and out in 15 minutes.

So at least three (and often ten) times a week, I would drive to an executive's corporate headquarters, schlep my laptop and projector into his conference room, set up my egg timer, and wow him or her with a fast-paced highlight tour of digitized video, animation, transitions and at least a half dozen peeks at multimedia programs we had built for others. Usually the combined effect of all this motion on his oversized screen and my non-stop narration resulted in this senior executive calling some of his other staff in to look at the show. When that happened, I typically shut up, and let them dialogue about all the ways they could use this new technology "they had been reading about."

An Easy Sell—A Scary Realization

Whenever appropriate, I would interject some Internet statistics now and then, that bolstered someone's position that they had to have an online catalog, website, or any number of other tactical E-Business tools. More often than not, I would leave with a group of high-level decision makers wanting more, and a list of Internet tools that they wanted us to propose doing for them. Of course, I was elated. Here we were, a little six- to ten- person company (the number varying depending on cashflow), being asked by giants like May Company, Mallinckrodt, Monsanto, Bausch and Lomb, and dozens of other Fortune 500 level corporations to propose E-Business systems that no one else in the Midwest was even thinking about!

My excitement usually lasted most of the drive back to our office in "The Barn." By the time I was walking up the stairs to our loft, that same fact rose over the horizon of my mind in a more ominous light, and it dawned on me that I had just agreed to propose "E-Business systems that no one else in the Midwest was even thinking about!" Yikes! How in the world were we going to pull this off? A good portion of the demo I was showing them was a hodgepodge of multimedia programs we had built in Macromedia Director for CD-ROMs or laptop use, but not online. Sure, we had Internet samples, but back then it was pretty dry stuff, and most of the dialogues in those executive conference rooms focused on doing things that were on the leading edge of the industry at the time—things they were usually hearing about in the IPO section of Marketwatch. Like any good salesperson in a first meeting, I had said that I thought we could come up with some solutions to deliver their dreams, and would have a proposal back to them in a few days.

It wasn't the proposal part that I was worried about. It was the content in the proposal. The part of the proposal that said we actually could build them the shopping cart system, or the virtual building tour, or the virtual sales meeting and online conference that they had to have.

Our Secret Weapon

Fortunately, on the technology side, I had a secret weapon - my partner, David. I don't know if we ever formally agreed on this, or if it just evolved on its own, but as early pioneers in Internet solutions our synergy came down to what David described as simply this: "If a customer wants it, we'll figure out how to deliver it technologically." Usually that meant starting with a clean slate, and designing the entire solution from the ground up, laying down original HTML hard coding and creating screen designs ex-nihilo— out of nothing. There was no Frontpage back then, no Dreamweaver or WebSphere or ASPs to make the building process easier.

David and the team usually came through with amazing first time solutions using the newest technology available, but that was only part of the answer. It wasn't sufficient for me to go back to the client and simply say: "Trust me. David will figure it out." Even though that essentially was what I knew would happen, the customer wanted more. They wanted a process they could watch, and feel like they had some control over. They wanted to be sure early on that they hadn't just agreed to let some little company in an old two-story barn in St. Louis County build something so new and radical that they were going to get burned.

I understood their concerns and their needs. We were

essentially digital architects, designing and building one custom Internet "home" at a time. No plan design was the same as the other. It was as scary as it was scintillating, but how could I reassure them that we really could deliver this new Internet construction?

Then it hit me. I had been here before. It *was* construction.

Think Of A Construction Project

Over two decades before, I had stood on an empty lot in Kirksville, Missouri, holding a blueprint of the new Wendy's building that was scheduled to open at that very location in just ninety days. I had never supervised a building project of any kind before. I had never worked with contractors in any capacity. Though I did have an Engineering degree, as I would later remind my dad at least once a week, it was an Aeronautical Engineering degree! I might have been able to tell you how to turn those blueprints into a decent paper airplane, but there was no way I knew how to turn them into a commercial building.

But over time, and with the help of just about every subcontractor on that job, I learned that you didn't have to know how to pour concrete, erect steel, or lay conduit in order to project manage those same disciplines. If you simply made sure that the logical progression of jobs happened as scheduled and that one part was completed in time before the next part in the chronology was to begin, you could end up with your building being finished on schedule, and open for business on your target date.

When I started referring to our Internet projects as construction projects and began managing them in the same way I had managed the Wendy's project in Kirksville twenty plus years before, two things happened immediately. First, our programming and design teams began to work together in new ways, with more efficiency. Second, and equally important, our clients immediately began to feel more at ease, and more confident that we knew what the heck we were doing. Sometimes even when we didn't at one particular moment.

The analogy still holds up today, and I still use it and

hear clients quoting it.

"We're not going to start hanging the wallpaper on your site until the conduit is in. It makes no sense to put up the drywall and paint before the pipes and plumbing are finished." "They won't bring the furniture into our online community until we've signed off on the rooms. It's much easier to move a wall when there's no clutter in the way."

We've gotten to the place where we have our clients sign off on every stage of construction. Though not blueprints exactly, we ask them to sign the schematic before we write the first line of code. They sign database designs, interface designs, and a bevy of other elements long before we have the respective specialists work on the project. No contractor in his right mind would start pouring concrete before the plumbing was in and approved. We're the same way.

Here's my point: I have never been skilled at any programming or development skill necessary to build E-Business systems, and you don't have to be, either.

While that system of selling and building everything out of thin air served us well in the foundation years, it is abjectly deficient today because of the incredible increase in options now available. There are hundreds of pre-built modules and components that you can buy or rent that can be up and running in just minutes. Most E-Business builders have solutions on the shelf that they've built with open architecture, and which can be reused for other customers with little effort, but the basic principles of building that we developed back then are still the struts and supports of every project we do today.

Many Options For E-Business Help

Everyone today, it seems, knows someone or is related to someone who says they do something with E-Business. The options and approaches to finding the tradespeople and specialists to help you develop and maintain your E-Business system are numerous. Most of them can be very helpful for portions of specific projects within your E-Business enterprise. On the other hand, many of them are dangerously ineffective and expensive if left to themselves, or if given the exclusive responsibility for the whole of your E-Business enterprises. We'll look at the main ones here, in that light. My primary goal is this: When you reach the end of this chapter, you won't be tempted to give any single firm or category the comprehensive exclusive license to build and manage your Internet endeavors.

My secondary goal in writing this section is to encourage you to take the reins of your E-Business development without concern for lack of E-Business experience. In order to get us there, it's important first to take a look at some of the most popular categories of outside vendors which organizations have historically turned to for help in the past. Characteristically, because of limited experience in the ever-changing E-Business environment, and a backlog of work, most promise a little more than they can deliver and deliver that which they *can* deliver a little later than expected. Each does, however, bring a different slice of the pie to the picnic, and may have the flavor or style that fits your needs at a particular place or time in your E-Business process.

Option I
Contracting with Traditional Business Consultants

"You know the old adage about owning a boat? How you might as well throw your money down the toilet, put your head in after it, and flush?" Chris asked me, spearing a piece of lettuce.

"Yeah. You end up smarter, wetter, and a lot less poor," I said, recalling the joke.

He shook his head as he swallowed, then snickered, "I found something that wastes your money even faster than owning a Sea Ray. Hire a big consulting firm who claims to know how to transform your business for the new economy!"

Chris was a friend of mine who was a product manager for a Fortune 500 consumer products company, and before our salads were half-finished, he was emoting as only an Italian can, silverware in both hands punctuating his every word. "We signed them up for six months to start, and we're now in the fourth month. We've seen seven account executives from their firm come and go, each time necessitating that we bring the new person up to speed, essentially starting from scratch. They bill us for every minute. The E-Business strategy they presented last week, after four months, was basically a reformatted outline that I had given them weeks ago. Now with over $110,000 spent, we're still no closer to launching our online catalog than we were four months ago!"

Chris discovered too late that abrogating control and direction to a consulting firm of so-called experts in E-Business is almost guaranteed to produce bad results at a higher price than other options. It's an especially sour discovery when these experts have no more expertise than you or I have and their own firms are going through a revolution that is more dramatic than most of our businesses.

As John Ellis writes in *Digital Matters*, "If you talk to the leading consulting firms' partners across the United States, what you'll hear in their voices is anxiety—in many cases high-anxiety. The new Internet-driven economy has turned their world upside down and inside out."[1]

One of the main reasons they are so concerned is that for the first time in their business careers, if not in the life of their firms, there is an aspect of business for which they not only don't have any expertise (which in itself is not that unusual), but they also don't have any practical way of pretending they do.

"These days, the only thing that traditional consultants know for sure is that somewhere out there, Internet technology and new economy entrepreneurs are conspiring to make their lives miserable."[2]

7 Questions For Traditional Business Consultants Before Giving Them Your Business

1. Who are the people who will actually be working on our project, and may we see their resumes?
2. Are there any other of your staff or support personnel that we will be billed for, and if so, may we see their rates and resumes?
3. Please list all seminars, courses and outside training in E-Business development that these people have had in the past year.
4. What other clients similar to us have you done work for, and who can we contact in those companies?
5. What are the maximum costs associated with each stage or phase of your services to us, and will you put that in the agreement?
6. When is the latest possible date for the project to be completed, given a worst case scenario? Will you put that in the agreement?
7. Based on the date above, will you agree to a penalty clause, whereby every day that you are late, we get a reduction in fees?

Why miserable? Because you and I and thousands like us each day are collaborating and sharing our E-Business wisdom with no need for pricey consultants. That's why "...the traditional consulting model no longer applies. It isn't even close to the new reality of the Web. The traditional model said: 'We make a trade. Your money for our smarts.' The Web model says: 'We collaborate, and get smarter together as we go along.'"[3]

Even without a marketplace Richter scale, consultants can see a major tectonic shift in the business landscape that portends a shake-up of their status quo like they've never seen before. In most cases this is good news for us if we recognize it. It really isn't that hard to spot.

Think about it. If you're selling shaving cream in 1950 and the consulting firm you hire arrives by train and shows you how many different ways you can paint a billboard on a barn, never mentioning TV at all, you'd know these were not the guys to help you into the age of mass media. Yet for most of today's big consultancies, the founding partners and principles of their firms only know how to do it the way that got them there. This is old school business. You ask for experts in E-Business and you'll either get a youthful band of recent hires, or like my friend Chris, months of "strategizing" while they learn what to do on your nickel. Remember, this is a brand new industry, moving faster than any other game in history. The big name consultants have no more tenure in the Connected Economy than you do. In many cases they have less.

Lewis Pinault, a former consultant with Boston Consulting Group and later a lead consultant with Coopers and Lybrand, gave us a peek behind the curtain with his scathing book *Consulting Demons: Inside the Unscrupulous World of Corporate Consulting*. In addition to defining the industry in such illustrative terms as "efficiency drones," "headhunting cannibals," "surface-skimming masters of pretense," and "experts in no industry but the promotion of their own sales and well being," he also presents an insider's view of how little these so-called experts bring to their business clients.[4]

When it comes to delivering expertise, Pinault writes,

"The appearance of a controlled solution at the right time [is more important to them] than the actual fix," and, "One of the current tricks is to propose everything."[5]

Don't be fooled by that famous name or guru associated with the firm that you think is managing your account, either. "One of the key rites and rituals is for gurus to find a back-up person to do the actual work."

As my friend Chris discovered too late, the soldiers the consulting firm sends to work with you often don't remotely resemble the generals they initially sent to get your business. They also often don't know any more about your application solution than you do. In an article in *Business Week* entitled "First Sue All Consultants," Deloitte & Touche consultants were seen at Gore (makers of "Gore-Tex") looking "bewildered, constantly on the phone looking for direction from the technical support arm of the software company they were supposed to be experts in."[6] When each of these individuals from the consulting firm is costing Gore hundreds of dollars an hour to stand there and learn their craft, it's no wonder the company sued.

If you haven't guessed it by now, I am not a big proponent of giving the keys of your E-Business kingdom to a traditional consulting firm. You may be able to make a case for turning to them for specific portions of your E-Business project, or even hiring them for ongoing measurement and research (as long as you have quantifiable goals and fixed costs). For most organizations, however, short of the most experienced managers of Fortune 500 companies, or those whose board members' last names all end in a vowel, giving a traditional consulting firm all the reins will likely result in a very long, expensive ride to a destination that was never on your map.

Option II
Hire an IT Firm

Whether you are looking at an information technology team, an information systems company, or a computer solutions group, limiting their scope will be the the key to protecting yourself from a big mistake going down this trail. Whatever you do, don't assume that because E-Business uses computers and networks and information technology tools, you should give the reins of your E-Business development to an IT firm. They can certainly help with a portion of your E-Business system, but don't expect them to have any understanding about things outside of their traditional playing field.

I was invited to speak to a marketing organization not too long ago, and I shared the platform with a relatively successful principal from a local IT firm who had built some E-Commerce pipes for the heavy metal industry. I knew a little of his work, and was one of the many in the crowd looking forward to his insights. When it came to getting a program built and delivered on time, he was one of the best. Unfortunately, when it came to communicating to an audience of business owners and marketing executives, he fell prey to the temptation that most brilliant technical professionals yield to when asked to speak; he gave them technical brilliance.

It took only about fifteen seconds for me to tune out. I was with him up until his title slide dissolved into the very first topic, "25 Network Protocols You Must Set Up Before Starting."

Although he was allotted twenty minutes to present, by reason of my vantage point on the stage, I could see that he had over eighty powerpoint slides locked and loaded into his laptop, which I presume contained the exhaustive compilation of everything he knew about building a web project from scratch. I say presume because he didn't get past his fifth slide before time ran out, coincident with audience members running out as well. To

> **5 Questions To Ask An IT Firm Before Giving Them Your Business**
>
> 1. Who are the individuals that will be working on our project daily, and what is their background and experience?
> 2. Besides IT courses and training in programming, what E-Business courses, meetings, seminars, or round-tables has this staff attended in the last 12 months?
> 3. Please show us five representative projects that are online right now, what your team did and did not do, and what the costs to the client were. Please provide client contact names so we can talk to them.
> 4. When it comes to site design, the look and feel of pages, navigation protocols and the like, what role to you play?
> 5. What work does your firm do besides E-Business projects? What percentage of your time and income do they account for?

say his presentation was boring would not only have been an understatement, it would have missed the bigger issue. In my experience, except for skill-specific web design and software courses created for the developer or coder to improve his or her programming acumen, most owners and operators of today's businesses and organizations are not interested in learning the fourteen steps to animate a .gif file.

Computer solutions firms are great at what they historically said they did best—providing talented people who are skilled at information technology with the solutions and programs to fix or improve in-house systems. What they are usually not so good at is what many have falsely claimed they are—that by reason of their computer expertise they are by default E-Business experts.

As Mark Mehler noted in his Opinion section of *ZDNet*, many have found this to be true in practice. "Two unsightly varieties of weed threaten to overrun the garden of delights known as the E-Commerce solutions market. Overpromises and underdelivery are the unfortunate outgrowths of...inexperienced vendors and neophyte business purchasers who are riding roughshod over normal IT purchasing disciplines."[7]

Mehler cites the Giga Group research which issued this blistering assessment of the IT solutions providers: "We believe the risks of failed IT engagements are especially high in E-Commerce today."[8]

While there are probably many exceptions to this rule, and with time, many success stories to the contrary, the traditional outside IT or IS company is not ideally suited to be the sole developer of your E-Business system, simply because E-Business is much more than the technology.

Take a look at the services provided by a typical IT solutions firm, and you'll usually see what I mean. Most are presented in, as well as rooted in, the environment of digits. Here's a sample of a promotional piece of a typical one:

"We specialize in COM/DCOM, Distributed Internet Architecture, N-tier Client/Server, CORBA, Java, ActiveX, Active Server Pages, Site Server, Commerce Edition, HTML, DHTML, XML, Microsoft Visual Studio, Visual C++, Visual

Basic, Visual InterDev, Visual J++, Microsoft Transaction Server, Microsoft Message Queue, Oracle Designer/Developer 2000, Oracle JDeveloper, PowerBuilder, Inprise JBuilder, Windows 2000, Windows 98/95, Windows NT Workstation, Microsoft SNA Server, Server, Windows 2000, Windows NT Server, UNIX, HTTP, LDAP, TCP/IP, Microsoft SQL Server, Oracle, and Sybase."

You get my drift. Whether programs, tools, operating systems, database management, or other similar terminology, these groups are incredibly skilled at what I call pipefitting and connecting. That is, they are concerned with the structures and frameworks of the system, but not so much with what goes through the system, or how it looks and feels going through the system.

Let me relate it to another technology every business uses, and which every manager has to ensure is working at the highest level--your telephone or the voice portion of your in-house communications system. Like your E-Business enterprises, the telephone touches customers and employees alike. It can present your organization in a good or bad light depending upon how it's used, and it is active twenty-four hours a day. Now, imagine with me, for just a moment, that your local telephone company installer comes into your office one day complete with tool belt and cable, and says he wants not only to pull the wire and hook up the phones at the receptionist's desk, he also wants a contract to write your customer service strategy. Wouldn't you get a grin out of a Moe Howard concept like that? You might as well ask your accountant to make sales calls! Knowing how to connect the phones does not mean one knows how to *answer* phones, deal with customer problems *on* the phone, or encourage a field rep *using* the phone.

Check the IT staff's resumes, and they will confirm my theory. They usually studied programming and integration, with all sorts of IT and IS focus. Few studied E-Business. Even fewer studied consumer behavior in the Connected Economy, or commerce in a borderless marketplace.

When I was feeling my way through my first Wendy's building construction project, I didn't have any experience coordinating the erection of a retail establishment. I certainly didn't understand how the plumbers made the water run uphill, and the poop flow down, but I can tell you one thing. I didn't ask the plumbers to handle installing the menu board and intercom system for the drive-thru. Not only was the "drive through" concept a new one, the idea that a qualified pipefitter would have any notion of what a customer's expectation was at the speaker would have been ludicrous. It would have made no sense. It would be like asking the concrete foreman what I should say in the newspaper ad. These specialists are a God-send for doing jobs within their fields, and in the right context.

Even though he brings in a ton of money every Labor Day, you don't ask Jerry Lewis to *manage* the MDA. Likewise, you shouldn't ask an IT firm to manage your E-Business strategy.

Option III
Contract with a Traditional Advertising Agency

Now we're swinging the pendulum to the other extreme. While the traditional ad agency will likely have a much better sense of the connected customer and E-Business concepts in general over the aforementioned IT firm, their abject lack of technological growth and speed to change in the '90's has left them playing catch up today. As the cover story of *Fast Company* so succinctly stated, "Speed Wins."[9] A typical ad agency's relaxed pace can be problematic if you give them authority over the grand design or management of your full E-Business program.

As Robinson-Humphrey's study showed, with ad agencies leading the way in the old economy, it took Coca Cola twenty-two years to build its brand, McDonald's fifteen. Yet in today's economy, Yahoo! established its brand in just two years.[10]

Don't get me wrong. There are numerous traditional agencies who have bought Internet development shops to accelerate their curve, like Roger Yount has done with Brighton USA. There are others who have banded together to share their E-Business development skills and tools, essentially pooling resources in order to help other fellow agencies that need E-Business solutions for clients that they may not have. Worldwide Partners, for example, is an elite group of some of the world's top advertising agencies (usually the best shop in each major city), who make their fields of specialization in E-Business available to other members and their clients expressly for this purpose.[11]

A good number of traditional ad agencies however, are still mired in their roots, inextricably tied to tools and philosophies that are not ideally suited to the Connected Economy today, or to your E-Business development. They typically deal in currency that takes too long to cash, and that loses value faster than you can spend it.

Rewinding the tape a little to review their history is probably important here. Traditional advertising, marketing, and communications companies hit their stride in the 1950's, in the post war boom that saw not only boomers like me birthed at an accelerated rate, but also witnessed the first consumer generation. In previous decades before World War II, the U.S. led the world in manufacturing. The historians called this the Production Era. People bought products because, simply put, they were produced. The folklore we read about today was true then. You could have a Model T in any color you wanted as long as it was black. Frigidaire produced one color ice box, and later refrigerator, because they could sell every one they made in white without having to add color versions to their production line.

Things changed after the war, when good paying jobs for a whole new middle class of Americans meant more disposable income to buy more things. Things that they started hearing about on radio, and seeing on TV. Things that had features and benefits and luster and polish. Things that had new options, colors, and shapes. American consumers, like moths, discovered their attraction to brightly lit things that promised to make them feel better, happier, or warmer in the winter.

As competition increased, the companies who manufactured these products began to allocate increasing budgets to advertising, differentiating their products from competitors products that often looked, tasted, or felt just like theirs. Need to sell more cigarettes? Have a celebrity do a spot extolling the health benefits of a Lucky Strike, and watch sales spike the next day. The major television networks in those days often could guarantee 50% or more of all Americans watching TV would be tuned into their "Show of Shows." Put a similar ad in *Life Magazine*, and reach even more smokers. Sponsor the "Game of the Week" on radio, and know that one out of two G.I.s that started smoking while overseas was listening.

Without getting too much deeper into history, I think you get the point. It was a media-based, media-driven specialty. Advertising was birthed, nourished and sustained in the '50's, '60's and '70's by producing ads. That may sound painfully obvious to you now, but since the 1980's, while still generating increasing revenues by producing more and more ads, most advertising agencies have gone to great lengths to try to convince you and me that they are not in fact, ad producers.

I should know. I've not only had numerous opportunities to hire agencies, I had a short tour of duty as a vice-president of an ad agency in Kansas City in the early '90's. Two of our current core companies, Brighton Interactive, LLC and TrainingDepartment.com,live under the same roof as, and are corporately part of, the Brighton organization, which until late 1999, was known as the Brighton *Agency*...one of the Midwest's top

8 Questions To Ask An Ad Agency Before Giving Them Your Business

1. What jobs do you do best in the E-Business environment, and what jobs are better handled by others?
2. Please provide detailed resumes on all your staff who will be working on our project, and highlight E-Business experience.
3. Besides creating great site design and presentation excellence, what else are you proposing you are qualified to handle for us? Why?
4. Besides traditional media, what other online advertising have you placed for clients, and what were the results? Do not include banner ads.
5. Of all the awards you've won last year, which ones were attributed to E-Business assignments or modules? Why?
6. Please provide case studies of at least three clients for whom you have developed one-to-one e-mail, site personalization, or customer-capturing and customer relationship systems, and the results.
7. Who is heading up new technologies and new applications research in your agency, and what initiatives are you developing for your clients with regard to 3G and the wireless web?
8. How do you measure success in these kinds of projects? Would you be willing to tie a portion of your fees to reaching measurable objectives?

advertising agencies. Why the push toward diversification? Why a focus on all of the marketing mix, as opposed to just ads? In a word, survival.

By the early 1980's, traditional advertising was getting hard to pull off. Over the years, concomitant with the exponential increases in TV stations, FM radio stations, magazines, and other mindshare bombardments into the heads of consumers, advertising and marketing communications firms realized their media foundation was getting sliced in smaller and smaller wedges. Getting bang for the buck was more difficult. Their corporate customers, many of whom were going to marketing seminars and reading books by authors other than Ogilvy and Trout, began asking for other tools in the marketing mix.

Here's their little secret. Despite all the measurable successes that direct mail had in the 90's, or one-to-one direct is having today, and despite the power of e-mail to deliver more measurable responses per dollar invested than any other tool, ad agencies still love to talk about their creative. They still love to show off their ads. They still decorate their walls with awards for print and TV campaigns that show well. If you doubt this, just check any issue of *Advertising Age*, and see what is featured. You can even look at its sister publication, *Net B2B*, launched in 1999 as a spin off specifically for the Internet world, and you'll see that Internet sites are presented and evaluated based on visuals.

What does your agency talk about? Do they say how they successfully increased one-to-one e-mail ROI by adding more variable fields, and how they delivered database-driven order data from client's websites to their salespeople in the field on wireless, or do they talk about the new creative idea they had? If they are like most, they are still talking about advertising, and waxing about a digital revolution that has already passed them by. As late as May 2000, in promoting one of the main gatherings of leading advertising agencies in North America, the AAAA summarized the meeting by saying:

"This year's two-day program will feature client and agency perspectives on advertising creativity and discuss the implications of digital communications on advertising agencies. The AAAA will also present its annual O'Toole Awards for creative excellence."[12]

Discuss the implications of digital communications? Present awards for creative excellence? If this was 1992, maybe, but October of 2000? Come on! It's after reading things like this that my mind goes to what former Secretary of State Dean Acheson said: "Time spent in the advertising business seems to create a permanent deformity, like the Chinese habit of foot binding."[13]

The reason I take the time to bring that background to the foreground is because in my experience the question of their roots is one of the key barometers you must use to determine what role, if any, your ad agency will take in your E-Business development. Are they still doing and talking about the historic ad agency roles? Then use them for those tasks only. Traditional advertising isn't going away. In fact, it's increasing, as more and more online businesses realize the value of a broad marketing mix.

If they have made the jump, invested in the Connected Age, hired E-Business professionals, and are committed to the transformation of their business along with everyone else's, then perhaps they can be used for your E-Business development in greater roles and proportion than the average traditional agency.[14]

Option IV
Give the Job to a Web-Design Firm or Boutique

Although many of the web design shops that were birthed out of someone's garage or basement in 1994 have either been gobbled up by one of the aforementioned organizations or gone out of business, there are still a significant number of independent, largely local firms battling on.

While a few of the survivors made the jump into the big leagues, and were rolled up, morphed, or merged into larger Internet companies that were birthed in the heady NASDAQ-driven '90's, those remaining shops that sustained on a local or regional basis into the 21st century had to have something positive going for them.

For one, by sheer tenure alone, they probably have more

experience and understanding of website development than the other types of firms mentioned above. Moreover, you can pretty much guarantee that the people who own this business and survived have developed the skills of tenacity and flexibility that building websites demands.

Lastly, and maybe most importantly, they likely have become expert at one or more programs that currently make the Internet hum. Whether it is a facilitating program like Dreamweaver, which makes the building of web pages faster and easier, or an accelerating program like Flash, which makes user experiences feel more like interactive movies, they likely have some serious learning curve hours behind one or more of today's tools. This is where boutiques come in, as individuals who have followed this course decide to specialize in one or more of these elements, and rent their services to others who need that specific skill.

On the other hand, these folks are not usually ideally suited to strategizing, designing, or building a comprehensive E-Business system, precisely for the same reasons. If you've become an expert at web design, or are prolific at an Internet development program, you are not an expert at E-Business strategy. You can't be. You wouldn't have had the time to learn it. It's also probably not in your nature.

I learned this the hard way years ago when my

8 Questions To Ask A Web Design Firm Before Giving Them Your Business

1. Who are the people who will actually be working on our project, and could we see their resumes?
2. When it comes to modules like online catalogs, shopping carts, E-Commerce and the like, do you write the code for us from scratch, do you have a system already built, or do you use an outside solution?
3. Please list all seminars, courses and outside training in E-Business development that your staff has had in the past 12 months.
4. Please show us five representative projects that are online right now, what your team did and did not do, and what the costs to the client were. Please provide client contact names so we can talk to them.
5. When it comes to site design, the look and feel of pages, navigation protocols and the like, what role do you play?
6. What added value do you bring to the mix over all the other options, including ASPs?
7. When is the latest possible date for the project to be completed, given a worst case scenario? Will you put that in the agreement?
8. Based on the date above, will you agree to a penalty clause, whereby every day that you are late, we get a reduction in fees?

company was swamped with work, and we simply did not have enough bodies to go around. On a particularly busy day, we had some clients drop by without an appointment, and I was forced to delegate another mini meeting to a new member of our development team, Tom, who had come to us after owning his own web design firm for a couple of years. I figured with that background, he'd be able to easily show the client our marketing audit documents, explain the process, get him to sign off on it, and be finished in less than thirty minutes. It was to be an easy meeting done at the conference table without a hint of technology. At least that's the way it was supposed to work.

An hour after I had left him, I found him hunched over his workstation, staring at the screen muttering, "Come on, come on!" The client was looking at the screen as well, and the marketing audit paperwork was no where in sight.

"Did you show Dale the marketing audit?" I asked.

"Huh? Oh, no. Not yet," Tom replied, still looking at his monitor. "I thought he'd like to see the latest push technology from BackWeb. It's really cool, but this thing is being stubborn!"

"You haven't done the marketing background paperwork yet?" I asked again, forcing a smile.

"Uh, no. It's uh, over there. Come on, come on, you animal! Quit torturing me!" he replied, to no one, I assumed, except his computer...who was now apparently purposely irritating my new developer.

"Tom, don't speak anthropomorphically to the computers," I said, quoting an old line, "They just HATE that."

That snapped him out of it, and he turned to me and the client and simply said, "Oh. Sorry."

The reason Tom was not inclined to do a marketing audit, and chose rather to show Dale, our client, something on his computer, goes to the heart of the problem you'll have if you delegate your E-Business program to a web design firm or boutique.

Those that were gifted enough to become web designers in the '90's, and survive as such, are not as a result, the people who are gifted to manage E-Business in the 21st century.

As online commentator the Net Prophet said: "The Internet is about creating customized, personalized relationships with customers...Webmasters can't create [these] because they are not marketers."[15]

We have to remember and constantly remind ourselves that we are not building a website for our organizations. We are not managing another project in the same genre as the annual tradeshow, this year's benefits package, or the sales training program. E-Business is not another item we are going to do, it is something we will do, on an ongoing basis, for the rest of our lives. E-Business is not just another strategy in our business plans, it is THE strategy, and THE business plan. Your Internet systems are not one link in your organizational chain, they are THE links to every organization in your chain.

As Scott Kirsner reflects, "In just a few short years, the Web has become an indispensable part of daily life for millions of people around the world. It has reshaped the logic of countless industries...But within the next few years, the Web is expected to make the greatest impact yet."[16]

He goes on to describe the resources and investment Ford, Toyota, and other auto makers are putting behind their E-Business systems, with enough detail and context to clearly illustrate that E-Business is their only business plan for the future. Add to that the overhead view of the plants Microsoft and Intel are building in Finland, in proximity to Nokia, and you'll get a new understanding for how comprehensively connected the very near future is going to be for all of us.

With that kind of macro view in focus, it probably goes without saying that you should not give your business future over lock, stock, and barrel to a web designer only.

Option V
Hire a New E-Business Services Firm

Call them E-consultants, Internet services hybrids, strategic Internet consultants, I-integrators, or a host of other names of the week. These web-only companies started appearing in the late 1990's in part due to incredible demand. This demand comes when organizations realize they must join the Connected Economy, they need help doing so, and they don't feel confident in any one of the options we discussed earlier.

Not surprisingly, "E-Business only" firms often have a good cross section of skill sets, with staff members that have come from traditional consulting firms, ad agencies, IT solutions groups, web-design shops and more, now bound together with the twin cords of E-nomenclature and E-profits. Some of those that have had some momentum include the well-funded and similar sounding USWeb/CKS/MarchFirst,[17] iXL, Scient, Sapient, and Viant. Then there's Fort Point Partners, Proxicom, HomeCom, Cambridge Technology Partners, Diamond Technology Partners, Agency.com, and Transaction Information Systems. In Europe, there's Icon Media Lab and Nua. My favorites are the reptilian variants, Razorfish and ThunderLizard.

They'll tell you that because they are E-only (or "I" only, depending on what's in vogue at the time), and because they have more practical experience in Internet and E-Business development (which in many cases is true), they are the only people companies can turn to for the complete E-Business implementation.

These groups that exploded onto the landscape in 1998 and 1999 by doing strategic Internet programs for such major public brands as E-Trade, British Airways, Compaq, K-mart, Met Life Insurance, Sprint, and Texaco, now have a niche that all of the other E-Business service providers discussed above have a hard time penetrating.

All things being equal, if you had to pick just one group to give your E-Business development to, and cost was not a factor, you'd probably be best served by one of these new firms. If you're like me, however, or any of the managers and owners I usually hang out with, cost is a factor. That's where you can get creamed going down this avenue.

Like DeBeers with diamonds, and the Saudis with oil, these Internet-only specialists have managed to carve out a pretty decent oligopoly for themselves, and seem to be able to price their services at incredibly high levels. What's funny about that in many cases is, until around 1998, these same people were doing the same thing they're doing now for 90% less than what they charge today! It's almost as if they just added zeroes to their pricing ledger.

As Eryn Brown explained in an article in *Fortune Magazine*, "They used to be those geeks who designed your Web pages. Now they're 'Web strategists' running $100 million consulting firms."[18]

Take New York City's E-consultancy—Agency.com— which until around 1997 was building webpages for around $50,000 each, all inclusive. Today, the group will charge as much as $30 million per project, and ring in up to $500,000 just to produce an exploratory report.

According to Chan Suh, the CEO of Agency.com, that's just the beginning. "Our first year was infancy. Our second year was childhood—who do we want to play with? Our third year was high school. Last year we had our freshman, sophomore, and junior years in college. Now we're being kicked into the real world."[19]

Suh asks for and gets $500,000 minimums by writing forecasts, strategies, competitive reviews, and opinions about software suppliers. As of 2000, he had over 600 employees devoted to this new breed of Internet-only consulting, with offices in Boston, Chicago, London, Paris, San Francisco, and other cities.

Razorfish is another "garage to gold watch" story. Started in 1995 with a handful of employees and a dog, today this New York based NASDAQ organization has over 1,400 staff-members. Sound like there might be a little more overhead to cover, now? Listen to Michael Simon, Razorfish's EVP:

"We are aggressively maintaining the same culture we had when there were only 18 employees. We still have the dog, we still have the guy who plays with Leos, but we also have a lot more personnel. Things are just on a different scale."[20]

I had an opportunity to see one of these new Internet-only firms in action, when one of our clients asked us to help them launch their online training system.

To reach a new consumer market for one of their

commercial products, this St. Louis-based Fortune 500 company decided to launch a brand new Internet system to be built from scratch, and the director, Ben, had chosen one of these aforementioned mega-consultancies to do the job in its entirety. Well, almost in its entirety. They held out one portion of the package for us to do. The online training module.

In a pre-planning meeting Ben revealed in general terms what it was costing him to have the E-consultants do the job. "They're going to fly in five people, rent an office down the street, commute back and forth for six months, with time billed in excess of $300 per hour per person. That's just the group that's here with us. There are another dozen people at their home office, coding the thing around the clock, to meet our deadline."

I waited until I got back into my car before I used my calculator. Let me save you the trouble. It was over $3 million dollars.

From Ben's perspective, that was a good investment. He was very confident that an entirely new E-Business brand and system would be built and running in six months or less. He had no internal staff to help him do it, so he had to outsource completely. In his mind, because every month the site was delayed could potentially cost his company $1 million in lost revenue, he had to go with the fast, expensive option.

---

10 Questions To Ask An E-Business Agency Before Giving Them Your Business

1. How are you funded? Do you need to make a profit this year?
2. How does a project or company like ours fit into your company goals and ideal client mix? Compare us to an ideal client.
3. Who are the people who will actually be working on our project, and could we see their resumes?
4. Are there any other of your staff or support personnel that we will be billed for, and if so, could we see their rates and resumes?
5. Please list all seminars, courses and outside training in E-Business development that these people have had in the past 12 months.
6. What other clients similar to us have you done work for, and who can we contact in those companies?
7. If we only contracted with your firm for a portion of the job, like building site architecture or e-marketing only, how would you work and relate to our other vendors?
8. What are the maximum costs associated with each stage or phase of your services to us, and will you put that in the agreement?
9. When is the latest possible date for the project to be completed, given a worst case scenario? Will you put that in the agreement?
10. Based on the date above, will you agree to a penalty clause, whereby every day that you are late, we get a reduction in fees?

I likened it to the businessperson who takes the last seat on the Concorde from New York to Paris to close an account, or the product manager who decides an hour before the tradeshow opens that paying those electricians $275 to plug your booth in isn't as expensive as it seemed yesterday. If you have to have it now, you'll pay more.

Parenthetically, I have to confess that when I finally met the famous five that had flown in from New York and Atlanta to build Ben's site in six months, I was a little surprised. It wasn't their youth or their dress that concerned me. I learned years before that those things are meaningless in the E-Business trenches. It was their abject lack of communication skills. They didn't make eye contact during conversation and a few had an unnerving habit of typing on their laptops while they spoke.

I remember when we had our first (and last, it turned out) joint meeting with Ben, the five from this firm, and our team. The purpose of the meeting was ostensibly to decide how our online training component was to integrate with their yet to be built E-Business site. We had some proprietary concepts that we wanted to keep proprietary, and Ben really wanted our system, but because the New York guys wouldn't sign a confidentiality agreement, the dialogue was strained. After a number of false starts, I finally brought the subject to a head.

"Look, we signed a confidentiality agreement, but you've said you won't," I said, addressing the leader of the gang of five, who was both typing into his laptop, and, curiously, repeating what I was saying softly.

"...signed a confidentiality agreement. We won't," he whispered, keys flying.

"That tells me that some of our proprietary concepts could be in jeopardy," I continued.

The echo came again. "...proprietary concepts in jeopardy." Click click click.

"So I think as far as we're concerned, this meeting is over," I said, and stood up to leave.

As the rest of my team followed suit, we all shook hands, had short sidebars with Ben, and then simply walked out of the conference room. When I got to the door, I turned to the typist, I guess still hoping to make eye contact. He didn't look up.

I listened. Sure enough, just above a whisper I heard him, "Activated Multimedia leaving Conference Room." Click click click.

I'm sure that today these folks are much better at what they do, and how they present what they do, but if you choose to go this route because of time pressures or other business demands, know that you are paying top dollar for a team of "specialists"—any one of whom a few short years ago might have been sitting in Mrs. Parker's Biology class trying to make a chicken claw give her the finger. So check the resumes and pedigrees of the actual staff working on your project.

Putting It All Together

In my experience, even if you have concluded that you need outside help, there still is a decision you must make. With all of the options before you as mentioned above, and all of the vendors expressing how much they can do for you, there is still the question of overall control. Most of the people discussed here will usually suggest that you give them the job of developing your E-Business almost in its entirety, and with it, the control. This is one option. In short, this is a decision to delegate and assign the entire scope of your E-Business development and ongoing growth to one of these aforementioned companies, and trust, hope, and pray that they know what they're doing and have the soldiers to pull it off. That's one option.

The other option is to do what you have always done. Don't hand the keys and the control over to an outsider completely. Instead, oversee the big picture and assign portions and aspects to a variety of specialists who can deliver as members of a team that you manage. That's the other option, and the one I recommend.

My clarion call and message to you is simple. If you choose to use outside vendors, firms or specialists to help you with your E-Business development, go for the latter. Do what you've always done, and manage this enterprise as well. There will always be things about E-Business which we don't know. So what?

Too often, we're tempted as business leaders and managers to think that an acknowledged lack of ability in E-Business programming translates to a lack of ability in E-Business building and managing. If you only read *Internet World* magazine, and listen to your IT guys exclusively, it's hard to think otherwise. They're convinced that E-Business is 99% programming, coding and other "magic" to which they have the secret passcodes, and you don't...so leave your E-Business to the "professionals." That hasn't been valid in any other area of your business life, though, has it?

Talk to your CPA for over thirty seconds and you'll hear the same kind of lingo-laden, exclusive-club mumbo jumbo. It may remind you why you never wanted to take advanced cost-accounting, and why you hired her, but it never stops you from directing her and expressing your expected outcomes. Not being trained in accounting never prevented me from working with, or managing, accountants. It just eliminated accounting as one of my top 1,000 career choices.

I still don't know the first thing about the complex world of worker's compensation, but it doesn't prevent me from working with our worker's comp attorney, and articulating in no uncertain terms that I don't want to pay that extra fee the state just tacked on to our filing.

Ross Perot built what was at one time the largest computer processing company in the world, yet the closest the CEO got to computer programming was in approving the hiring of a programming manager.

You can be sure that Carnegie never knew how to spill a stream of slag, but that didn't stop him from hiring people who did, and managing the process so effectively that he built the largest fortune of anyone in his era.[21]

Don't get me wrong. The technology that's behind the Connected Age and frictionless economy isn't pedantic, and it's certainly not static. It's just not the central issue for organizational leaders that some like to make it. You and I might not know how the pipes are made, and that's okay. The trick is to know, like Carnegie did, that you can hire pipe-makers, who can mold and shape the technology to fit your needs.

As Larry Pearle of EcomAdvisors said, "Often a website falls in the hands of the technology person at a company or the guy that runs around and fixes the computers. The website is a marketing piece. It should be headed up by people who understand marketing."[22]

As I have stated before, I have gone out of my way to ensure that I not get sucked into the temptation of learning how to program Internet pages. I have maintained from the beginning that as revolutionary as E-Business is, it still is business, and can still be successfully harnessed, managed, and maintained by average members of the organization like you and me, who know nothing about writing code.

You don't have to get your hands in the mortar, to direct and manage the building of a retaining wall.

Someone may say, "Well, if we are not physically laying the bricks, and we don't want to know the details of bricklaying, how can we be sure the wall goes up on time, according to good engineering principals, within budget?"

That's where your management skills come in, and the ability to turn to experts in E-Business for those specialty skills that you don't have or want to have. The trick is knowing which experts to call on, for which services.

Looking for help starting from ground zero? Breakaway Solutions is a new breed of outsourced resourcing that specializes in delivering a team of experts and executives who can jump start an online presence, and then hand it off to you as a viable entity. "Breakaway's virtual management team consists of technical, financial, and marketing people at the VP level...for the rented guns, the ability to kick start a new company brings its own reward."[23]

There are a number of similar firms now appearing in cities like London and New York. To route them out in your area, try starting with your leading placement and executive recruiting firms. For example, in St. Louis, a call to Grant Cooper and Associates will connect you with a local office of Bridge Corporation, which, as the name implies, does this kind of E-Business launch bridge work.

Like construction projects, each E-Business development will require different specialists. Yours may have more or fewer than mine. By way of illustration, this chart lists the typical experts in their fields that I call upon when building or adding to an E-Business development, and how I like to pay for their services.

E-BIZ TASK	TYPE OF EXPERT NEEDED	PAYMENT
Strategy	Enlightened Traditional Consultant or E-Business Consultant	Per Project
Infrastructure	IT or IS Firm or In-house IT—Pipes and Hardware Only	Ongoing
Back End	Internet-only Developer—Database and Coding Only	Per Phase
Site Image/ Design	Web-Design Boutique/Digital Artist Freelancer—Look and Feel Only	Per Page
Site/ Extra Sparkle	Internet Specialist Program-Specific— Customer Experience Only	Per Project
Site/ Special Features	E-Business Tool Maker—Paste and Use Only	Per Tool
Fulfillment	Outside Connected Fulfillment House —E-Transactions Only	Per Order
Advertising	New or Traditional Ad Agency with dot-com Experience/Resources	Per Campaign

This listing is not exhaustive and is only illustrative. Obviously, as new innovations come to the forefront, you may need to add a new category of expert for a specific portion of your development, much like the construction foreman does as building designs change. (For example, as this is going to press, I am adding a new hybrid cellphone/PDA/wireless expert to my team, because so many of my clients will be there soon.) This is just an example, but it does give a good snapshot of the kinds of experts to have on your team.

It also can be illustrative of a hierarchical order of development of a new E-Business system from scratch. While some of these areas of focus can be done at other times, and within other order contexts, I've found after managing scores of new projects from ground zero, both as designated foreman for clients, as well as managing E-Business projects for my own companies, that this hierarchy works reasonably well.

For those who have determined that the large part of your E-Business development efforts will involve managing vendors and subcontractors like these, it is wise to get more resources that address these challenges in more detail. Peter S. Cohan does a good job outlining his approach to E-Commerce project management in his book *E-Profit*, and it's definitely a good investment if you are pursuing that specific construct. Even if you are not exchanging or selling products or services online, his approach is worth a brief look.[24]

Depending on your view of the future, part of the logic behind how you collect and manage your E-Business team can be categorized into short-term and long-term perspectives. Some may have a more limited view of how wide and far the Connected Economy is going to go or impact their organization. My personal opinion is that we are still only scratching the surface, and the future will be more Internet-centric than even the most optimistic forecasters have voiced.

If you're like me, and you believe in management according to the Wayne Gretzky school of goal making, you want to position your organization now, not where the puck is, but where it is going to be. When you look at the combination of the expanding availability of global computing and Internet access, the availability of affordable wireless broadband worldwide, and the exponential increase in customers and consumerism from large, formerly isolated people groups, you begin to see the writing on the wall. (If you like to track stats and trends like this, there are many online resources that keep pace with the growth of the Connected Economy worldwide. See Appendix.)

So how do you put your team together for both immediate E-Business development, as well as for the long haul? My recommendation is to pick the best you can find within your budget for each category, and manage them like a construction supervisor manages his subcontractors, only maybe with less screaming.

There are numerous other resources in print and online. A number of the sites listed in the Appendix have significant libraries of articles and courses on managing your development that are a simple search away, downloadable, and free.

Before you rush out to line up these outside vendors, if for no other reason than to use it as a leverage point in your negotiations with them, you may want to take a few minutes with the next chapter. For a significant portion of businesses and organizations, excluding perhaps only the Fortune 500 few, the new E-Business building solutions described in the pages that follow could be the ultimate answer to your Internet enterprises now, and for a long time to come.

Interested in your own E-Commerce site, customized the way you want it, for only $30 per month? Read on...

13

DO IT YOURSELF WITH ASP "APPS ON TAP"

Imagine this scenario. You are a new merchant at your local mall. You've secured a 2,000 square-foot location at the top of the escalator, and the empty space stares at you, demanding attention. You may have a great product line, but you still need to have the space fitted with racks and displays in order to merchandise properly, and the whole store has to be designed and furnished for maximum traffic. You secured bids from interior designers, retail equipment wholesalers, furniture distributors, cash register suppliers, credit card vendors, and the rest, and you are thrilled that you were able to keep the cost of setting up your store under $75,000. You talked to other merchants in the mall with similar-size spaces who paid a lot more than that to build their shops, and you feel like you're getting a good deal.

You are all set to sign all of the contracts to spend your $75K and get your store design started, when you see the owner of the new fashion shop across the way. She just finished building out her space, and since it looks great, you pop the question. Now imagine your shock when you hear her answer.

"Well, it looks like a $75,000 job, you're right, but I found a turnkey store design builder who set the whole thing up for free, and who only charges me $30 a month to use it. I don't even have to sign a long term deal."

As ludicrous as that sounds in the context of a retail store in a mall, this is exactly the scenario that was made available to thousands of average businesses and organizations beginning in 1999. It signaled another dramatic shift in the way E-Business and Internet applications were to be developed from then on, and opened up even more opportunities for businesses and organizations of every size to get in the connected marketplace without spending a fortune. This incredible innovation is called the ASP model.

I first discovered the astounding world of ASP-based E-Business solutions late one evening in 1999, while poking around the Internet as a favor to a friend. As a one-person consulting company, John was looking for a quick and affordable way to simply put up a Web presence and allow prospects to leave an e-mail request for information. Because he specifically said he wanted it up and running sometime that week, and had absolutely no money at all to spend on development, I thought I'd see if I could hook him up with a local freelancer or ISP that offered low cost homepages. It was early in my search when I stopped on a listing that described a scenario I found hard to believe. The headline said it all: "Your own E-Commerce site with 100 products, only $29.95 per month." It was the first of what would turn out to be dozens of such companies we discovered who were offering a radical new way of approaching E-Business: renting a shared solution.

Until late 1999, for those who wanted to launch or grow their E-Business endeavors, the options I mentioned previously were pretty much exhaustive. You could mix the players or tools, and create hybrids of partially outsourced and partially in-house development. You could lean on consultants, or manage specialists yourself. You could turn the development over to an E-agency, or you could hire a web development boutique. What you really couldn't do was eliminate the prospect of someone somewhere spending some time building and developing your E-system through programming and software integration.

As the last months of the revolution century wound down, a new concept could be seen starting to form over the dawn of the millennium. Like the weather in Seattle, tools and solutions in the Connected Economy tend to change daily. A look at the horizon suggested there could be another dramatic innovation coming which would make it even easier for organizations of every size to implement E-Business, regardless of skill levels, budget, or size. It was a concept that for the first time, effectively eliminated the one factor that was unavoidable before—the need for someone to program and code the site. This new innovation of providing applications as online services had the potential of solving any of the remaining time or budget hurdles that were unavoidable until now. They promised to shake up the status quo, especially for those of us who were looking for faster and more affordable ways to do E-Business.

Fred Sandsmark puts it this way: "Any business that wants to set up shop online has to jump a number of hurdles...building the commerce infrastructure can easily cost $10,000—often a lot more. But now, no-cost and low-cost site-building companies hope to knock down some of these hurdles..."[1]

In the broad sense, an Application Service Provider hosts, distributes, and manages access to programs or applications through a centrally managed network, usually on an incrementally low-cost subscription or rental fee basis. Instead of spending time and money buying and installing an application on numerous hard drives or networks within the organization, companies are now letting ASPs provide those applications to their offices and their employees. In this way, you can access everything from simple CRM and office management programs with file and calendar sharing, to complex 3D modeling and enterprise-wide order-through-manufacturing systems that, until the ASP burst on the scene, required long-term commitments and huge up front investments.

The ASPs that have transformed E-Business for the average organization are what could more simply be called "apps on tap." These are the Internet site builder and store builder programs you can use for a fraction of the cost of all of the other options we discussed previously, with almost as good a result! Your E-Business site or module is built using programs or templates that reside on an ASP's server, with the ASP being responsible for making sure the program, servers, and your site work correctly 24/7. No software to buy. No servers or ISPs needed. No HTML to code. It's amazingly affordable, and eight out of ten organizations find it affords them all of the customization and flexibility they need.

To illustrate the importance of ASPs to the industry, let's look at one of the first E-Business site-building ASP models that gained significant early popularity—the Yahoo! store—and see why their value proposition sent shock waves through the offices of most developers.

The Yahoo! online store is a great example of big things coming in small packages, and for countless thousands of small business owners and organizations, has been the key to E-Business opportunity. In 1998, Yahoo! purchased ViaWeb and entered the biz-wiz market with a vengeance. Since then the Yahoo! Store system has seen its customer base balloon from 1,000 merchants to over 10,000. "The most important thing we've done...is integrate it into the rest of our network...primarily Yahoo! Shopping and the Yahoo! directory," says John Briggs, Director of Yahoo!'s E-Commerce.[2] Like similar packages offered by others we'll discuss later, building an E-Business online through the Yahoo! Store builder is as simple as typing, clicking, and selecting. When you go to the start page to build your Yahoo! Store, a simple overview screen greets you with as good a summary of the process as any I've found:

"Create your site on our server, using nothing more than the browser you're using to read this page. Build a store and start taking orders in minutes."

As we read further, we discover what thousands of others had during their first exploratory research on the Yahoo! storebuilder—that this ASP concept offered an almost unbelievable pricing structure. As of press time, the Yahoo! package was still saying:

"Yahoo! Store is a combination of an authoring tool and a hosting service...You build your store on our server, using an easy point and click interface...There is no software to install: all you need is an ordinary browser....We host your finished site...You can have your own address like www.yourname.com or you can use stores.yahoo!.com/yourname...Orders are accepted securely using industry-standard SSL encryption...You can retrieve orders (securely) from our server over the Web...Orders can also be forwarded to you by fax, or processed online..."

There's even more: "You can log in to change your site or retrieve orders whenever you want, from any browser...Pricing is simple: $100/month for a store selling 50 items, and $300/month for up to 1,000 items...There is no start-up fee, and you can cancel whenever you want....You'll be amazed how easy it is to create your own online store...You just enter information like the names, prices, and descriptions of the items you want to sell...It takes less than a minute to add a new item, and you can upload an image for it with a single click...As well as being easy to use, Yahoo! Store generates sites that are among the best looking and technically most sophisticated on the Web. See for yourself in some of our users' sites...There is simply no easier way to have a high-quality, secure online store."

To illustrate the significance and impact this new model brought to the market, look at what happens to cost. Since 1996 *netB2B* (formerly *Business Marketing*) has tracked costs associated with E-Business development and has been the guidebook for developers establishing their fees. For an average E-Commerce package that includes a site design, publishing tools to add and delete products and content, a shopping cart system and hosting, median prices averaged between $77,000 - $100,000.[3] Now, compare that to the package offered by Yahoo!. The $300 per month package provides everything that this custom site built the old way offers, with a lot less hassle. Even if someone makes the argument that the Yahoo! E-Commerce package doesn't allow you to build a completely customized look and feel (although it does have thousands of design options), how many would feel that it was worth shelling out $70K for that slight difference alone? If this was your company, would you think the price was worth it?

For eighty percent of the market or more—those not in the music, footwear, or advertising business where your site is essentially a streaming commercial—the answer has to be "no." Consider Carol Higgins. During the day, Carol worked as a desktop support engineer. At night, she built a new business. When her one-year-old start-up, Binky Computers for Kids, needed an online presence, she followed the path many of us have also followed.

She purchased off-the-shelf Internet development software, spent about three months trying to learn the "easy HTML programming," and after hundreds of hours ended up with a poorly designed, sputtering, amateurish-looking site that was essentially an online brochure. If she did manage to get a site visitor interested enough to make a purchase, they had to e-mail or phone the order in. "Putting up an Internet storefront on my own was frustrating," she said, "and I [work in] information systems." Then she discovered an E-Business store-builder ASP, and after just a few hours, had a fully functioning, awesome-looking 23-page Internet store, binkypc.com.[4]

Like other industries have discovered with products and services that predate the Internet, renting is attractive to the consumer. If someone makes staffed office suites available by the week rather than committing to a long-term lease, there will be a market. If a company is offering the customer the ability to rent the truck by day rather than buy it, especially when the customer is not in the moving business, it will be extremely attractive. Over a million people have decided to pay monthly for Call Notes from their local telephone company, rather than owning their own answering machine.

It is the combination of not having to own hardware and software, and of off-loading the responsibility for keeping them current and maintaining them in a 24/7 marketplace, that has made the ASP growth curve go through the roof. Stewart McKie puts it like this:

"Simply hosting the application software remotely is only part of the job...the ASP has to perform a role that combines the responsibilities of an ISP, a traditional outsource service provider, and a value added reseller, (VAR)."[5] The Yahoo! Store, like most ASP packages for E-Business customers, offers a host of benefits, advantages, and value propositions that make it attractive to so many organizations. Which of the following benefits are important to you?

Reduction in Talent Cost

In the late 1990's when unemployment was at an all-time low, finding and hiring E-Business programmers was a full-time job, and an expensive proposition. No matter how high or low unemployment goes in the future, technology talent will remain one of the most costly segments to staff, so any scenario that mitigates that fact can be extremely attractive to most organizations. ASPs are knights in shining armor in this regard. When the application provider is a well-known, financially sound organization with a strong background in the industry, leaning on their talent pool makes sense financially, as well as creatively. You can then free up your in-house teams and outsourced talent for other jobs that have more mission-critical urgency and bigger payback.

Reduction in Innovation Cost

How much time has your staff wasted researching software trends and comparing applications? It's difficult today for top management to ensure that their own staff stays on top of all the technological improvements and developments birthed within their organization, let alone keep pace with the endless lists of providers of same. With the ASP model, the latest innovations and upgrades to your application are made automatically at the provider's end, by the ASP provider, with no effort or thought on your part. The ASPs have a vested interest in keeping your application as current as innovative as it can be, so innovations are frequent, and upgrades usually automatic and cost-free. Because your ASP agreement usually is a short term, month to month commitment, if you do find a better offer, moving is painless.

Reduction in Software Support Cost

Anyone who has purchased applications knows there are many costs associated with the software which impact your bottom line beyond the price of the application itself. Software must be installed, tested, and integrated with your systems and platforms, both initially as well as on an ongoing basis with upgrades. By eliminating all these peripheral costs associated with applications, your "rental fees" to use applications offered by ASPs are even more economical, because of the recovered time and costs no longer devoted to supporting the software in-house. Your team needs to invest nothing more than the time it takes opening the browser to have the program up, running, and current.

Improved Security

ASPs lead the industry in applying the latest security features to their systems, and invest heavily in protecting you and your clients. They know that their future viability depends on their maintaining the highest level of protection, so like a bank with thousands of customers, their vault is bigger and badder than any one individual's could practically be. By allowing the provider to invest in the tools and technologies to keep pace with potential threats, you ride on their coat tails vicariously.

Increased Speed of Deployment

Almost all of the apps on tap that allow you to build and launch your E-Business site, store, or system today are real-time integrators. Make a change to a page, add new products, or completely overhaul the look and feel, and with the click of a launch button, the site is changed and made live on the Internet instantaneously. Because these providers are up and available 24/7, you are not limited by the schedule constraints of others in order to affect your changes, and can adjust and tweak your E-Business system daily, or even hourly, at will. And the best part is, in most cases, you can do this as much as you want, with no additional charge. That business and industry have awakened to the benefits of ASPs is clear. Research by Zona in June of 2000 summarized it well. When asked why they found the ASP solution so attractive, respondents said it was because of "reduction in cost of application ownership, the ability to focus on...strategic business objectives, and the freeing of IT resources."[6]

There are other benefits that make the ASP model attractive to many organizations. Please see the Appendix for more information on other ASP sites and their benefits.

Had ASPs been available when we were designing and building E-Business packages for our customers and ourselves, I'm convinced that a significant number could have been solved beautifully through an ASP solution.[7] There are just too many upside benefits for average applications. Sure, there will always be a place for the super-custom, super-complex E-Business packages, the unique corporate Intranets or the large-scale Extranet assignments, but for the majority of the time, ASPs can fill the bill.

There is no question that ASPs in general, and the site-builder and storefront-builder biz-wiz apps specifically, exploded onto the market—and surprised many. As recently as October 1999, *Business 2.0's* usual pollyannesque view of E-anything was constrained in an article entitled "Web-o-Matic." The article is worth reading even today, and presents some interesting perspectives on the subject through some killer interviews. But clearly they had not seen the Tsunami coming, and remained at best ambivalent with summaries like: "In the end, it's tough to say who's taking the greatest leap of faith: the small businesses that are hoping a suite of prefab tools can transform them into savvy E-Commerce players, or the free-commerce companies that are counting on the success of those small businesses."[8]

Regardless, most understood the significance. In an article in *Red Herring*, Monua Janah described ASPs' benefits and future importance in terms that even Sir Thomas More would appreciate. "In Utopia, software doesn't exist...The lure is that the customer, whether an individual or small business or Fortune 500 corporation, never has to deal with the complexities of installing and maintaining software, [but can] use it all by paying a subscription fee."[9]

That ASP models are the wave of the future is clear, when you recognize that even the traditionally slowest tortoise in the race, "big blue" has jumped into the act. Go to any of the IBM public sites and you'll see that they have ASP site development and ASP commerce packages, similar to that which Yahoo! (and most of the industry patriarchs), offers, for a low monthly fee. Add to that the fact that Microsoft is putting full weight behind its .net enterprises, and the future seems certain.

Traver Gruen-Kennedy, chairman of ASPIC (an ASP Consortium), put it this way: "The simple fact is ASPs are on the rise in every wired country in the world, with Japan taking a lead role in the development and cultivation of outsourcing centers. Australia is another international bastion of the application service provider, as the country's traditional role as an isolated location fades."[10]

Today, you can find everyone from FedEx[11] to Intel[12] offering us an opportunity to use their ASP model to do business on the Internet, for little or no investment at all. On July 10, 2000, Intel Online Service, the Internet application hosting subsidiary of Intel Corp., announced the availability of AppChoice Managed Hosting Services. "Designed for customers who want control of their mission-critical applications, AppChoice also brings forth the benefits of a fully managed, outsourced hosting solutions. Intel Online Services currently has five data centers, with a sixth scheduled to open within the next month in India. Overall, the company intends to invest $1 billion by the end of 2001 to develop and integrate Internet data centers worldwide."[13]

So what does all this mean to you, and what kinds of E-Business packages and services can ASPs bring to your organization? In a word, a bonanza. The Yahoo! store-building package mentioned above is just one of scores today who offer similar or more expansive ASP packages in the E-Commerce category.[14]

Since Yahoo!'s national ASP site builder launch in 1998, there have been dozens of biz-wiz companies added to the marketplace, offering similar or more innovative versions and systems.

Following are some of the most popular or most promoted E-Business apps on tap or ASP biz-wiz services available for consideration.

14

ASP REVIEWS AND RATINGS

Application Service Provider-based E-Business builders exploded into the marketplace in late 1999 and early 2000 with scores of new names and familiar names anteing up their branded versions of these popular "apps on tap." The result is a veritable buyer's market, with enough "biz-wiz" products for every organization, need, and budget.

The E-Biz site builders, store builders, and EZ-Commerce systems that follow are all 100% browser-based, listed alphabetically, and are reviewed and rated using the ratings key at the end of the chapter.

addAshop
addAshop.com

This hybrid site-building storefront system may not be the best choice for the organization focusing on developing a professional E-Business site *sans* shopping cart. Yet for those who are looking for an extremely fast-to-market, low cost E-Commerce site builder, addAshop has packaged a tricked-out system that almost looks too good to be true. They bill themselves as the premiere site for easy turnkey E-Commerce that only takes five minutes to set up, and they do make it easy. The addAshop group does not ask you to pay for anything to start, and they'll manage the inventory and shipping, process credit cards, and provide customer service; all at absolutely no cost to you.

What's the catch? None really, as long as you don't mind stocking your store with *their* merchandise. The addAshop system is essentially a series of conduits for products, credit card services, and other supplier's wares along the distribution chain, with one of their numerous channels being a virtual storefront that has your sign on it. What that means is if you are a travel company, you will select the "Travel Store" option in the site-building process, and addAshop will automatically stock your store with "sightseeing guides, travel videos, suitcases, etc."

You'll do this, according to addAshop, for the commission that ranges from 5% to 25%. If you want to make more than 25%, you have to sign up for what is called "Premium" service. This is for those who want "absolute control over their merchandise's pricing and who wish to determine their earning potential." Before you run out and start spending those commission checks, you should know that this "Premium" service will cost you $9.95/month, or $99.95/year.

If you can get past this circuitous approach, and don't mind the ground rules, you may be refreshingly surprised with the ease and facility the addAshop system serves up. Granted, the addAshop site builder is limited in both layout options as well as designs, but you'll get through the five-step process in five minutes or less, just as advertised. When it comes to personalization, you'll only be given a few choices. You can drop your logo in, name your "shop," and write a short welcome message. There's even a "logo builder," for those who like 3D fonts. In five minutes or less you'll end up with your own shop, stocked with the merchandise that is offered in the addAshop chain. You'll also see some buttons and links that you didn't create or select, including newsletter, live support, and others. Through the administration menu, you can access reports, product inventories, and the wizard to change or modify your store.

If you have your own ideas on design, your own products, or a communication style that mandates inserting the word "choice" into sentences as frequently as Al Gore, this package is definitely not for you. For those who don't mind the low amount of customization and control, and who want to get online in the fastest way possible, addAshop is worth a look.

	Cost	Tools	Designs	Look	Feel	Extras	OVERALL
addAshop	$	••••	•	••	••••	••	•••

Alcamall
Alcamall.com

This clean and easy to load site is the kind of presentation you would develop if you knew you had to deliver across a variety of platforms around the world—and with offices in Malaysia, and Asia their target market, that's exactly what parent company GO2020 did. According to their PR, GO2020 intends to be Asia's first and leading provider of integrated ASP service, and offers a pretty cute little E-Business building app. Alcamall offers an E-Business package it calls "your one stop E-Commerce business center," although somewhat light on features, can handle the average need.

The challenge lies in the fact that GO2020's mission in general is somewhat nebulous, and the verdict is still out as to whether this online system will be a long-term player. With the system currently being offered for "FREE," and charges accruing only in the form of transaction fees and subscription fees, the amounts of which are not clearly spelled out, it's hard to tell what the system would ultimately cost. Add to that Terms and Conditions that give no assurances that anything you load into the system will be be protected, this one currently remains higher on the risk scale.

	Cost	Tools	Designs	Look	Feel	Extras	OVERALL
Alcamall	$	••	•	••	••	•	••

Amazia
Amazia.net

Here's a site that doesn't waste time cutting to the chase. Amazia calls itself an "Application Service and Content Provider" and the slogan remains ubiquitous throughout. Under Amazia Solutions you are quickly taken to an elliptical graphic that gives you one-click navigation to anything you want to know about their program. Though not the most cutting-edge graphically, the pricing section, for example, has the meat of the matter in large bold print, the third line down from the top: "Your cost is only $74.95 per month," and goes on to explain what the package includes.

For those that want the facts without a lot of fluff, this site tells it straight up. Amazia charges no set-up fees or transaction fees, only the monthly fee. If you sign up for 10 months, at press time Amazia gave an extra two months, free. This basic package includes up to 300 items in a "store," with the next upgrade to 1,000 items an extra $50/month. The scale continues up from there, and apparently thinking big, even allows for those with as many 250,000 items.

	Cost	Tools	Designs	Look	Feel	Extras	OVERALL
Amazia	$$	•••	••	••	••••	••	•••

AT&T Small Business Hosting
ipservices.att.com/sbh

When I saw the half-page advertisement in the Business Journal that said, "Take my business online...and give me an E-Commerce store! ...For as little as $25/month," I was excited. When I looked at the kicker and saw the AT&T Small Business Hosting name and logo, I was thrilled. My thinking was, if AT&T is in the biz-wiz business, we might see some real innovation now. Unfortunately, it hasn't turned out that way yet.

There are three problems with this freshman package geared to the Small Business. First, as much as it tries to stand on its own, the site still is clearly and inextricably joined at the hip to the bigger AT&T world that is in the business of pipes, backbone, VPN tunneling, and the rest. That the URL advertised begins with "ipservices" is not happenstance.

Second, though long on explanation and featuring some of the most detailed charts in the marketplace, there is no easy direct way to see sample sites, layout options, or even a glimpse at the site building tools. In the FAQ section you can glean that there is an "I-Store Wizard" for beginners and an "I-Store Pro" for more experienced users, but not a single screen grab or illustration is offered.

There is, however, more than enough detail on costs. If you favor a system with a lot of pricing levels and options, you'll like the AT&T site. Level one includes 40Mb of data and 2Gb of transfer per month for $25/month. Level two ramps up to 60Mb and 4Gb respectively, for $50/month. Level three provides 100Mb of data storage and 6Gb of bandwidth per month. All three have a $50 set-up fee.

If you move to the E-Commerce arena, you'll pay a $75 set-up fee, and then increase your monthly costs based on the number of products on your site. For Level one sites, you'll pay the minimum of $50 per month for up to 20 products, $75/month for 100 products, and $115 for 500 products. Level two sites will show $60/month, $85/month and $125/month for the same product numbers. Level three sites will pay $125/month for up to 100 products, and $210/month for 500 products features on the E-Commerce system.

Thirdly, and perhaps even more problematic, is the fact that you'll have to jump through the AT&T hoops of registering yourself, ordering or redirecting your URL, and signing up for one of their packages before you are allowed to see the system and tools at all. Even then, you are not given instant access:

"Your account is created immediately after you order service. Our automated system allocates space on the server and creates your exclusive password and login IDs. The entire process takes less than a day to complete. In many situations, you can be creating a site within 30 minutes of signing up for service."

With so many site and store builders available to the Small Business today with open access, sample sites, free trials and instant useability AT&T's guarded presentation and slow process may be too much work for many. Hopefully in future iterations they will have revised that approach. Until that happens, this one is probably interesting only to a very patient few.

	Cost	Tools	Designs	Look	Feel	Extras	OVERALL
AT&T	$	••	••	•••	•••	•	••

bCentral from MSN
bCentral.com

If there ever was a question as to the benefits of having Microsoft follow early innovators into new markets and enter the competition, this classy system could illustrate the answer in technicolor. bCentral has taken the most popular features from the Yahoo! Sitebuilder, added a few of their own, and then put the Microsoft weight behind their ASP package. But in so doing, they didn't lose sight of who their customer was, and made a concerted effort to avoid any appearance of big business bias.

The first indication that Microsoft knows who you are comes when you first go to the bCentral homepage, and the header loads up "Online Services for Small Businesses." That's significant, since that masthead is there for any and all pages in the entire MSN Business section. Beneath it, under a few standard menu items at the top, comes an amazingly clean three column layout with headers that read "Start," "Market," and "Manage." From any of those points, you are just one click away from some of the most customer-centric, nuts and bolts presentations in the market. Using bottom-line questions like "How does it work?" "Show me some samples," and "What do I get?" bCentral lets you review, test, and evaluate the packages with amazing exigency. Compared to some others, it feels like lightspeed.

The standard package to "take your business online" is an affordable $19.99 per month, and includes a selection of over 40 design themes and templates, and 40MB of space. While bCentral promotions also suggest an unlimited number of pages allowed in your package, they cap your bandwidth consumption at 3000MB of data transfer per month.

There are some other strategic advantages the bCentral system affords users that are also unique to the Microsoft system, and they all start with the word Microsoft. Building your site using this system automatically qualifies you for listings and placement in the MSN family of sites and portals. The administration system to build and manage your site comes with some prebuilt equity, too. First-time users will find pull down menus and navigation very similar to other Microsoft products like Word.

Yet probably the most valuable feature of all is the simple fact that you are on a Microsoft ASP system, and that says a lot. Even before ASPs were defined as such, Microsoft's then version of Moneycentral was providing a 100% browser-based portfolio management tool for thousands of investors around the world. Since then hundreds of thousands of users have been added to the system, and it still ranks #1 in its class.

The only downside to the bCentral app is ironically the flip side to the Microsoft brand advantage mentioned above. Even though they have scores of templates and an almost infinite number of color and design options you can select, the final basic product looks a little stiff. There are ways to get around this, including using FrontPage within the site, but in my mind, that takes us out of the box of a pure app on tap builder.

For those who don't mind sporting a little Microsofty look and feel, who are looking for a one-stop online shop to build an E-Business site with full commerce capability options that can grow, this is a very sleek, affordable choice.

	Cost	Tools	Designs	Look	Feel	Extras	OVERALL
bCentral	$	••••	•••	•••	••••	•••	••••

BigStep
BigStep.com

BigStep cuts right to the chase the moment you log on, and makes the value-proposition clear. Headlines and slogans like "Build Your Business on the Web" and "Where E-Business is Everybody's Business" underscore their formula. As of press time, the company said it this way: "Use Bigstep.com to create and manage a website, market your business online, sell products with secure E-Commerce, promote events, display a portfolio, send e-mail newsletters, and more. Most services are FREE."

BigStep's free services include using their site builder to build and maintain a site with unlimited pages, up to 100 items, and up to 12BM of storage space. Like most who offer commerce, if you want to accept credit card orders, you'll need to apply for an online merchant account. BigStep suggests using Cardservice International. You pay nothing to apply. After you're approved, you'll pay Cardservice International $24.95 per month and a 2.35% discount rate for Visa/Mastercard transactions, plus $.020 per transaction.

BigStep's site builder is easy to use, with little more than pointing, clicking, or typing needed to design your site. It also allows for a wide range of creativity and customization, including being able to pick that *exact* hue from a color wheel of infinite choices. The site is loaded with case studies and tips, showing how others have used this award-winning system to create a custom-looking site for a low, package price. It has a professional, high-quality feel without being snooty, and is decidedly *pro* the small business owner or operator. Real world samples range from "The Chile Fix," "eCandlestore," "10,000 Miles for a Cancer Cure," and a band site called "Idiot Box," which uses BigStep's system to sell their CDs online, as well as offer MP3 downloads.

With a motto "where E-Business is everybody's business," it's difficult not to like the BigStep approach.

	Cost	Tools	Designs	Look	Feel	Extras	OVERALL
BigStep	$	••••	•••	•••	••••	•••	••••

Concentric
Concentric.com

Here's another national hosting group that has diversified into other products that reach other markets, and although it's a little tough to find within their expansive site, Concentric has a site builder that may be worth a look.

Right off the top you notice their positioning strategy, and it's a cute bit of differentiation that may be attractive to those who want a little more help in the design architecture portion of their site building system. Instead of the usual templates with styles and color choices that form a frame for your own graphics, text and images, Concentric's version comes pre-loaded with text, photos, and graphics. That might sound ludicrous at first in the context of a "custom" site builder, but Concentric's approach is interesting.

You start by picking an industry that is close to your business. From there you quickly jump to the design section, replete with pre-loaded text and images that are *representative* of the end result. But you don't stop there. Concentric's builder directs you to replace them with your own content and company-specific graphics. The result of these machinations is a site that Concentric says "retains the professional look" of the model site.

If you want a fast, simplistic, almost thought-free app, this may be your system of choice. Currently advertised at $19.95/month, with the usual free month, Concentric's system is all there for you to see. If you like their templates, and prefer a minimal amount of creativity and control, you can jump into this one quickly. If you are one of those who can't find a design match, or who doesn't find Concentric's designs consistent with the image you want to project online, the current package may not meet your needs.

Concentric does offer upgrades in space and hosting packages, including the "Host E-1" product at $44.95 per month, and $50 set-up fee, which would be required if you wanted to offer commerce. This includes an EC-1 electronic commerce package and a CH-1 Web hosting plan, off-line credit card transaction processing, up to 25 products organized in up to 3 product departments, 100 MB of disk space and 5 GB of monthly data transfer, and 20 mailboxes. Ramping up from there, the E-2 plan provides 100 products and 200MB of space for $79.95/month, $50 set up fee. The E-3 package provides up to 10,000 products, 300MB of space for $149.95/month, $195 set up fee.

	Cost	Tools	Designs	Look	Feel	Extras	OVERALL
Concentric	$	••••	•••	•••	••••	•••	••••

DXShop by DXStorm
DXShop.com

There's no getting around the attractiveness of packages that boast "Free Forever," but like the breakfasts in Las Vegas, and most of the other ASPs reviewed herein that make similar claims, you'll probably end up paying something in the long run. With DXShops that something will vary based on the number of products in your store, but if you know that going in, this one is worth a test drive.

DXShops is not to be confused with DXCart, or the parent company DXStorm, although the public site does mention all three. DXShop is the biz-wiz division, and apparently for the new visitor who hasn't heard about the ASP phenomenon, its homepage shouts: "Nothing to download, nothing to install. E-Commerce enabled with a click of the mouse." If you like to read tables, the Dxshop information pages detailing features and benefits will be appealing, and the free trial is easy to launch and jump into.

The site builder engine is menu-bar driven, with options for novice users as well as what they term "Power Developers." Major categories include appearance, products, checkout, shipping, and most have templates that offer general layout schemes and colors, or pull-down menus from which you can select your preferences. It's relatively easy to get started, and once you select even just one of your site design elements, you can go to "Site Preview" and see a store configured, complete with a Welcome greeting. Admittedly, you really couldn't open for business at that point, because many of the variable fields still need definition ("Welcome to the [Company Name] Online Store. We feature products such as [product name] and [product name]"), but it does give you a fast start.

If there were a downside to the system it would have to be in the price/value proposition. DXShop does offer the site builder and up to 12 products for free, but from 13 up to 100 products, it's $50/month; up to 1,000 products, $180 per month. From the look of the sample sites DXShop features, as well as the templates provided in the store builder, the resultant site layouts and designs are relatively run of the mill. This would not necessarily be a negative for some, if the package was truly free. But coupled with a pricing model that for all intents and purposes is going to be at least $50 per month for most who have even a token number of products, it may cause some to pause.

For those who have a quantity of products that matches up well with DXShop pricing levels, and like the way this site builder works, this might be worth a serious look.

	Cost	Tools	Designs	Look	Feel	Extras	OVERALL
DXShop	$	•••	••	•••	••••	••	•••

e-BizBuilder
e-BizBuilder.com

Another catalog and commerce entrant into the "apps on tap" E-Business building business is this appropriately named provider. Once you log on to the site (don't forget the hyphen up front), you can jump immediately to the "Service Plans" section and find three e-BizBuilder options. All purport to include an "unlimited number of products" that are limited evidently only by "Web Space."

The site is clean and streamlined, and easy to navigate. Two aspects of the system however, should be noted. First, there is some confusion within the site itself as to whether or not this is literally an instant app. In one section linked to the homepage, the text says "With the Web Store Builder, you can create your professionally designed Web site in a matter of days." Underscore *days*.

Second, this system does lean toward your having to know some programming, both HTML and a photo editor. At one place in the introduction it says, "Though pictures are optional, e-Biz builder suggests to have pictures of your products on your computer, so you can import them into your Web Store. A knowledge of resizing and converting your image into a gif or jpg is a plus. If you need help digitizing or resizing your images, e-BizBuilder can edit them for $10.00 per image."

This might be a moot point for some, but it is a little different than the majority of the competition who go out of their way underscoring the *lack* of programming needed to use their systems.

The Basic e-BizBuilder package includes the "Automated Store Wizard," shopping, reports, SSL secure payments, even shipping modules, and 5MB of space. That's $35 one-time set-up fee, and $19.95/month. The Solutions package with 20MB and the Professional Package with 50MB both add some extra bells and whistles, and are $35.95 and $59.95 per month, and have a set up fee of $75 and $100, respectively.

	Cost	Tools	Designs	Look	Feel	Extras	OVERALL
e-BizBuilder	$$	••	•	••	••	•	••

eCongo
eCongo.com

If you believe the promotions, eCongo is the only game in town. According to the company, eCongo is "the leading E-Commerce ASP...and gives your small business customers comprehensive E-Commerce solutions, under your own brand, without the cost and delays of developing your own." At press time, however, the site had very little information about their advertised "free merchant account" beyond a page or two of text, and was woefully short on samples. In order to begin the process of reviewing eCongo, users are asked to complete a form that includes an agreement to their terms and conditions; a real turn-off for those of us who like to shop and compare before we agree to anything.

By the time you read this, they may have expanded their site and packages sufficiently for you to evaluate their offers. Until you can see samples, take a test drive, and read the fine print, this one is probably not an ideal choice.

	Cost	Tools	Designs	Look	Feel	Extras	OVERALL
eCongo	$	••	••	••	••	•	••

Estoremanager
Estoremanager.com

Trade publications began running full page ads for this E-Business builder in the third quarter of 2000, featuring a yellow notepad with a handwritten list of "E-Commerce Requirements," that detailed a catalog of 1,000 products, credit card processing, and the rest. Underneath the image was the sub-header, "Impossible? Not Anymore," and a pink note that said "starting at $149/month." The ad itself was not especially compelling, nor was the creative design. What is remarkable was the fact that so soon after the explosion of the ASP site-builder model, a company new to the marketplace decided on an advertising campaign based essentially on only features and pricing. As every Marketing 101 text will tell you early in the syllabus, the last thing you use to differentiate is price, and only then if your product has followed the life cycle through to commoditization. That estoremanager jumped to this stage so fast is illustrative of just how much competition there is in this category already, and how much leverage it gives us as buyers.

Once you jump into the estoremanager system, you'll discern a bit more about the advertising strategy, and why the campaign was so short on product differentiation—there really is very little new or innovative worth mentioning. Not that this stopped them from waxing on in copy. From the moment you start navigating through the site you'll notice the inordinate amount of text used on each page, to say things that others communicate with a sentence, a bullet, or an image.

The most remarkable aspect of estoremanager that does set it apart is the fact that once you decide you'd like to give this system a try, you are informed that your first step is to "Contact an estoremanager sales representative to set up your account." No, this is not the merchant account—that comes next. This is simply to begin the process. To their credit, I must mention that I did receive a call from an estoremanager salesperson the day after I explored their site, but by then I was long gone philosophically. When the salesperson asked me why I didn't want to continue with the estoremanager system, I simply said "You make it too difficult." To which he simply replied, "Okay, thanks."

Because we are limiting our reviews to those biz-wiz applications that are 100% browser-based and accessible without the need for outside software or outside staff, the current estoremanager system does not qualify. If the prerequisite of contacting an estoremanager salesperson changes, and the system builder offers free access in the future, updated editions will include a full review of the package.

	Cost	Tools	Designs	Look	Feel	Extras	OVERALL
Estoremgr	**$$$**	**N/D**	**N/D**	**N/D**	**N/D**	**N/D**	**N/D**

freeMerchant
freemerchant.com

Here is an E-Business package system that will get you to the game quickly, and with a relatively low, or no up front investment. As the name implies, FreeMerchant's value-proposition is rooted in their stated philosophy:

"freemerchant.com is free, so take some of the money you would have spent each month on E-Commerce hosting and spend it on promotion." As pedantic as that might sound to some, this really is a system you can jump into without paying a dime. They even let you know that they "don't even have a billing department." The way Free-Merchant earns money is through partnerships, and by referring you to some of their value-added service providers, So if you don't mind the occasional pitches, this may be a system with which you could live.

A quick tour of the site will lead you to numerous live samples of businesses who are using FreeMerchant, and you can find out most of the information you need from their FAQ section. The FreeMerchant approach to using their site builder is pragmatic as well, acknowledging that a ten-minute site is possible using their system, but not advised. FreeMerchant says, "You could build a fully functioning store in ten minutes, but why would you? ...I can paint my house in ten minutes, but it would look like a ten minute paint job."

Like many others, if you want to use the system for online commerce you'll have to sign up for a merchant account separate to the FreeMerchant package. That's probably what they hope most will do, but if you don't need the online shopping feature, FreeMerchant could deliver a workable site building solution that costs you nothing.

	Cost	Tools	Designs	Look	Feel	Extras	OVERALL
FreeMerchant	$	••	••	••	••		••

Freetailer by Excite
Freetailer.Excite.com

Like George Foreman's post-retirement return to the ring, it's always refreshing when one of the earliest patriarchs of the Connected Economy shows up to play, and takes a shot at competing. Even if Excite is not the same team or company it was when first launched, just seeing the name associated with an easy E-Business building system is nice.

Until mid-July 2000, the package Excite offered was called the Storebuilder.Work.com, and with this system, you had either a very small, or, at most, a medium-sized site builder. The Brochure Wizard, which offered a bare bones mini site that included only three pages (Homepage, About Us, Customer Service), was free for 60 days, and then it cost $20.95/month. The iStore Wizard was comparable to most in the middle range, pricing a store with 50 items at $90/month, no set-up fee. But in terms of product breadth and options, the Storebuilder.Work from Excite was relatively thin, and needed a makeover.

That all changed when they launched their new "Freetailer" E-Business builder, which claimed you could use their system with unlimited products, unlimited pages, shopping cart, secure payment register, and more, all for free. Their site and news releases made a compelling pitch:

"We strongly believe that you shouldn't have to pay for anything before you sell something. Very few portals and E-Commerce solution providers believe this, charging over $100 monthly even if you don't sell anything. Call us crazy, but we'd rather you spend your money promoting your store than on hosting your site. Other solution providers and portals offer a free start-up period that only lasts a week or a month. Our free offer stands for as long as it serves your needs. There is no pressure to buy into a monthly service upgrade until you—and your store—are ready."

According to the company, users also get 25 megabytes of storage, 1 gigabyte per month of data transfer, customizable storefronts, a virtual cash register, and shopping cart services for free. However, despite the promotion spin, it should be noted that the Freetailer system from Excite will, in all likelihood, still cost you something. In order to offer your products or services for sale, Freetailer has a "merchant account and payment gateway" where you must pay a monthly fee of $19.95/month, and a per-Transaction Fee of 2.49% +

$0.29, with a monthly minimum of $15. Also, there apparently may be a set-up fee, although at press time, Freetailer was waiving the set up fee for those who sign up within 90 days. The system also hits you up for fees if you need additional space. 40MB at press time was offered for an additional $30/month, and 60MB was available for $55/month.

The other charge that for many will be unavoidable is the $9.95 each month to *remove* advertising from your site. According to Excite: "Your cost for Freetailer: nothing. The trade-off: advertisements are placed on your site. If you'd prefer a store without ads, you can clear the ads from your store pages...$9.95/month." Excite's advertising in essence is funding your online system. Check out the samples. If you don't mind the ads, then the trade-off might be worth it. In my view, having banner ads cycle at the top and bottom of your pages that include cartoon bunnies pitching "e-mail kisses" and "e-cards" does not a good first business impression make. But maybe those banners don't impact you like they did me.

Having clarified Excite's definition of the term "free," it should be noted that their online site building system isn't too bad, if you don't mind the few extra steps it takes to get started. You'll first have to register as an Excite member, with one passcode, then as a Freetailer member with another passcode. That, in itself, isn't a big deal. The downshift happens after you complete the registrations and are told you have to wait "up to 15 minutes" for your account creation process to take place.

Once you finally get to the builder, the building process itself is streamlined, and allows you to build and launch your site without mandating your credit card information up front. You do have to pony up eventually if you want to move to online sales, but for simple site building, this is one of the most risk-free systems in the market. A nice side benefit if you do decide to move to the commerce mode is an automatic free listing of your products in the Excite shopping portal, shopping.excite.com.

For those who have checked out other online E-Business builders, you'll probably be underwhelmed with the limited design layout, template, and architecture options currently available to you on the basic "free" system. It seems at every stage of the process, you are shown "upgrade" options that *will* cost you more, but once you sign up for a test drive, you'll receive a nice surprise in the mail—a guide book and CD-ROM with more tips and tricks on using the system to its fullest. Adding it all up, if you don't mind Excite running ads on your site, don't mind a limited number of look and feel choices, and don't have anything to sell, Freetailer could really turn out to be *free*, and may be your best value today.

	Cost	Tools	Designs	Look	Feel	Extras	OVERALL
Freetailer	$	•••	••	••	••••	•••	•••

Gobizgo by Net Objects
Gobizgo.com

GoBizGo says their system is "a great way to get you going and growing online," and like many of the newer ASPs, have cut the fluff and fat out of their pitch. Using questions from the perspective of the first-time user, GoBizGo quickly answers concerns such as, "How can I build a site without any technical skills?" and "How can I make my site look professional, but unique?"

This is an E-Business building system that has targeted a certain niche in the marketplace—small organizations that do not require huge catalogs and the requisite space that goes with it. With one of the most intuitive navigation schemes and a straightforward site-building process, GobizGo will be especially interesting to those who prefer icon-based instructions over those loaded with text. There are over 100 templates, and though most are pretty tame, there is enough variety to reach a wide spectrum of tastes and preferences.

Judging by the range of samples shown, GoBizGo's system is pretty loose and unconstraining, and will accommodate long, scrolling pages and large images ganged by the dozen. Many of the samples featured were structured in this manner, with the resultant load times and navigation effort high on the scale. But if these less-than-perfect sites built by average folks proved anything, it was the fact that whatever your business or organization, whether artisan or professional, big corporation or sole proprietorship, GoBizGo will probably have something for you that fits.

Starter Membership is free and gives you 3 pages. Full membership is $19.95 a month with the first 30 days free, and includes up to 25 pages. You'll have to go to the Catalog Add-on package at an extra $20/month to include up to 100 items in your system, which the company says they load and store on your site pages, rather than in a database to call up later. Overall, GoBizGo is an efficient, intuitive system that will be high on the list of those looking for flexibility and good value.

	Cost	Tools	Designs	Look	Feel	Extras	OVERALL
GoBizGo	$	••••	•••	•••	•••	••••	••••

Homestead
Homestead.com

Homestead is another site building system that knows who its core customers are, and doesn't try to hide it. The opening page has a little ellipse that promotes the idea that you can "Build a Site for Teens," "Build a Site for a Hobby," "Build a Site for an Organization," and yes, even "Build a Site for a Business." It also is an affiliate subsidized (read advertising) system, and therefore promotes itself as "free."

To say the promotion portions of their system has a homespun approach would not be a stretch. Even the terminology it uses caters to the inexperienced: "Everything you need to build and publish your own Web site is right here—at your fingertips. If you can drag-and-drop or click your mouse, you can build a great website with Homestead. If not for the header at the top that said "Small Business," I wouldn't have concluded it had anything to offer the average company. Their site builder system is surprisingly confusing for a site that is targeting everyone from children to grandparents, and uses layers and menus that include over 150 "design elements." By the time you sort through the little illustrations that signify different things on your pages (a cellphone, a trophy, a child's block), and read all the instructions on how to use the system, you can't help but wonder if there isn't an easier way.

Because there are so many other instant site building

ASPs that *are* an easier way, for most businesses and organizations that don't have time to waste this is an unlikely first choice. On the other hand, if you love to learn new programs, and want to invest the energy it takes to getting there, Homestead may be an option.

	Cost	Tools	Designs	Look	Feel	Extras	OVERALL
Homestead	$	•••	••	••	••	••	••

IBM HomePage Creator
http://mypage-products.ihost.com/usa/en_US/

If there's one thing you can say about Big Blue, it's that they are definitely big, and the IBM entry into the ASP world of instant apps is not shy about showing off the mystique. The HomePage Creator site, once you figure out how to find it, is a delight to use, easy to navigate, and clean—which is exactly what you'd expect from a billion dollar company competing for your attention. Headlines like: "Fast. Easy. Cost-effective. E-Commerce," and first-person pronouns in navigation schemes ("I'm looking for...") make for an efficient tour and a quick evaluation.

Not to be outdone, IBM HomePage Creator offers five plans to the E-Business builder, ranging from Basic to Platinum, which they define and constrain according to a bevy of categories. In general, the basic plan gives you 5 pages and 12 items, 30MB in storage and 2GB in bandwidth for $24.95/month and a $25 set-up fee. Ramping up the offering scale, you can move to the bronze plan, which is 6 pages and as many as 24 items at $39.95/month and a $35 set-up fee. Following these are the silver and gold plans, with incremental increases all around. At the top level where they apparently run out of precious metals and space, is the platinum plan, at $200/month, and a $150 set-up fee. For that you get 50 pages and as many as 500 items.

The site builder itself is straightforward in approach, and uses the "family tree" metaphor to explain the process. With the IBM HomePage Creator, you have two categories of site elements—"pages" and "catalog"—which you can populate with content individually or collectively. It's simple point-and-click architecture that provides an average range of customizing choices, and is flexible enough to expand to large quantities of products.

As a biz-wiz, it does a pretty good job getting the first time user through the process, except for one point. In the fine print underneath the site's "Fact Sheet," you discover that transaction processing service is provided by an independent payment service provider, and that this provider requires that you have a merchant account. You also read that you will be charged fees by this outside company, and that the merchant account will cost you to set up as well, if you don't have one. This isn't unique to IBM, and is pretty much the norm for online transactions. But the problem is that you really aren't given details about the extent of these charges, or how to plug into these outside vendors.

Arguably, this is not inconsistent with many competitors in the market, and while some include these elements within their packages, many do not. So IBM hasn't really said anything that should be a surprise. The problem some may have with all this is that IBM doesn't make it easy for you to get to these outsiders. You're essentially on your own, with the only advice on the site suggested by IBM in this regard being "contact your payment service provider for more information." For those who came to the site *without* an already established merchant account or payment service, which I have to believe is the case with some, this essentially means an extra step or two.

Apart from that easily corrected convenience issue, as a reliable system with a good range of pricing options and the strength of IBM behind it, the HomePage Creator is a solid competitor.

	Cost	Tools	Designs	Look	Feel	Extras	OVERALL
IBM	$$	••••	•••	•••	•••	••	•••

iCat
iCat.com

ICat is one of the early pioneers of template-driven site building, having come from a number of different iterations and brand names that date back to the mid-1990's. Even before the Internet took off, the precursor company to today's iCat was helping organizations build CD-ROM catalogs using the same elemental pathways of pre-built templates and architecture. Unfortunately, iCat's competitive advantage and early entry into the market hasn't translated to a leadership position, and today as a division of Intel Online Services, the company seems in some ways like a reticent player.

The iCat system has over 25 customizable templates, a shopping cart, and options like Cybercash and design services. The basic program is said to be $49.95/month for up to 50 items, but you can't find this information easily on the site. They do a pretty good job showing their two lead products, the "Web Store" and the "Commerce Cart," with demos that are lean and concise. But for the average visitor, the lack of clear pricing and configuration information may be frustrating. At press time, iCat offered a store with up to 100 items for $99.95/month, plus a whopping $1,000 annual fee, with ramps up to 1,000 items at $249.95/month and a $2,500 annual fee.

	Cost	Tools	Designs	Look	Feel	Extras	OVERALL
iCat	$$$	••	••	••	••	••	••

IcSite
IcSite.com

Billed as an "Internet Storefront Solution," this system from Lairdnet Technologies was launched in 1998, and the site looks like it hasn't had an upgrade since. With a black background, and red, blue, and white reverse 12-point type throughout, this text-heavy homepage is difficult to read and understand. At the bottom of an especially long scroll of text the system lists pricing at $69.95 for set up, and $49.95 per month, but few details are offered.

A quick excursion to the system's demo site is telling. With a product catalog that features two products, a "Retro Phone" and a "Beautiful Vase," as the entire range of products in a Home Interiors "store," it's clear that the presentation of this system is mostly a facade. Whether or not it actually can deliver a working storefront online is still a question.

	Cost	Tools	Designs	Look	Feel	Extras	OVERALL
IcSite	$$$	•	••	•	•	•	•

Imagecafe from Network Solutions
Imagecafe.com

After watching newer start-ups capture markets and revenue streams in their own backyard in the 90's, Network Solutions saw the opportunity in the instant app market and jumped into the marketplace with a vengeance in early 2000. With some slick direct mail campaigns and a stripped-down payment structure, Imagecafe is attempting to make the launching of an E-Business site as easy as ordering a cup of coffee.

Imagecafe is structured like most in the field, with a site-building tool that places your template choices on their servers. Surprisingly, they also give you the option of using their site building tool and taking what you've created "to go;" that is, to another vendor's servers. You pay more to take it with you, but it's an interesting option nonetheless.

The basic package that is designed to get you in the door is a 3-page hosted site for $19.95/month. If you want it to go, it'll cost you $99. A 6-page site using the Website Manager Tool is $24.95, hosted; $199.95 to go.

What differentiates Imagecafe from the majority of systems is the quality of their template designs, and the range of options available. They claim that their designs are "developed by professional web designers with years of experience developing custom sites for businesses," and apparently they've brought some of that pedigree with them. With over 40 template categories, and as many as six layout options each, the likelihood that you won't find a layout you can live with is remote.

This is also a system that gets you down the highway relatively quickly. Their promotional materials boast a start to finish time of thirty minutes, but I was able to click through even faster. Sure, you could spend hours analyzing every template, design, and color option; but for the average user, that kind of intensity won't be needed.

ImageCafe's 1-Click E-Commerce uses CCNow to add credit card processing to any Image Cafe website design, and CCNow says they will charge no setup fees and no monthly fees. Another service that brings added value and caters to Small Business is their affiliation with "Paper Direct." With just a few extra clicks, users can order letterhead, envelopes and business cards from Paper Direct that matches the design of the site they've created at Image Cafe.

All told this is a slick site-building machine that can handle all the speed you can give it, without sacrificing quality.

	Cost	Tools	Designs	Look	Feel	Extras	OVERALL
ImageCafe	$	••••	•••••	•••••	••••	•••	•••••

MerchandiZer by HipHip Software
MerchandiZer.com

Leave it to a Miami-based organization to push the envelope on E-Business site creation apps. If you've been waiting for a biz-wiz that would make the boys at big blue blink, then MerchandiZer, by HipHip Software, is for you. Here's a store-building app that will likely have more features and options than you need, but one in which you will be impressed nonetheless.

Thinking about the borderless marketplace and global penetration? MerchandiZer offers easy translation of your page, module or entire into any major language, as well as VAT (European tax) calculations. Want to offer coupons or promotions online? This system makes it easy to give customers incentives to buy. Been reading Peppers and Rogers? MerchandiZer will let you greet customers by name, let customers track individual orders and shipments, and build their own order system to their unique preferences.

MerchandiZer is offered in three packages. The MerchandiZer basic product, initially designed for the sale of products and services to consumers in the small office and home office market, provides over 40 template styles, the shopping cart, reports modules, and language translation. MerchandiZer Basic supports up to 500 products and provides one free month of technical support via telephone, with unlimited e-mail technical support, for an initial set up fee of $150, and $79.99 per month.

MerchandiZer Gold, the company's new mid-range offering provides up to 5,000 catalog items, three free months of telephone support, extra features such as gift registry and gift certificates, and group pricing for $249 per month.

If you are really serious about moving products online, MerchandiZer Premium allows up to 500,000 catalog items (using load balanced cluster servers to improve online speed and reliability), unlimited free telephone support, and the rest for $499.99 per month.

The store builder system is menu driven, with scores of templates that allow you to choose how your products appear on the page, how they are priced, what size the image will be and more. Make no mistake, this is a system that is designed for users who have products to sell, and MerchandiZer is strong when it comes to that side of the equation. Arguably, it does not offer as many GUI devices or tools for homepage layout and design as some of the more site-oriented apps, but there is enough variety from over 30 themes, and scores of colors to allow for a wide range of customization. If you aren't convinced that MerchandiZer can give you enough control of design by way of the tour or free demo, check out some of the sample sites like Dole Pineapple, Super bowl XXXIV Merchandise, and the Magnolia Spa.

With other features such as image zooming (for those products that show better in larger formats), the ability to offer and sell downloads of software or music, and over 15 payment options in all currencies, MerchandiZer could be one of the top choices for any E-Business that is serious about E-Commerce in the connected, global economy. One other nice feature: once you sign on to the MerchandiZer site and fill out a quick wizard with your name and e-mail address, after a few minutes of exploring you may find a "live" help messaging window pop up with a HipHip support person greeting you by name. Michelem was my contact, and she was polite, helpful, yet not intrusive. Once I confirmed that she was indeed live, and not a programmed response (by asking her who the quarterback of the Dolphins is, and what time it was), I was able to ask a few questions and get quick responses. Even after I informed her that I was an author reviewing the site, she said, "We would still like you as a customer." A nice touch in an automated environment.

	Cost	Tools	Designs	Look	Feel	Extras	OVERALL
Mer.diZer	$$$	••••	••••	•••••	••••	•••••	••••

MyCart.Net
Mycart.net

The first thing you'll notice when you come to Mycart.net's homepage is how well this organization communicates their system's features and benefits to the average first-time visitor. Simply by looking at the illustrated screen grab next to the hostess, you quickly learn that Mycart offers a merchant account in sixty seconds, that the system can handle up to 10,000 products, that there is an "Inventory Upload Wizard," templates, and more. It's a super-effective presentation that speaks volumes in its simplicity. But they don't stop there. Once you get past the sizzle on the homepage, there is some serious steak behind it.

The quick tour goes on to illustrate the process of building your site and store with Mycart, and why they underscore the fact that it will take 15 minutes or less. It's important to note in this regard that Mycart includes the time it takes to secure your merchant account in that fifteen-minute window, an exercise that on some other systems is a much longer, laborious process. Mycart's 15 minute set-up time that includes the merchant account begins to look pretty attractive in that context.

According to the site tour, you'll invest 5 minutes on "Initial Set up," which includes naming your store and setting up some basic parameters. Step 2 is to "Select Payment Method," which includes "applying and receiving your Mastercard or Visa merchant account in 60 seconds, with no application fee!" The last step is to load in your products, either individually or using the Mycart wizard, which imports in quantity. The tour says that this three-step process will take you about 15 minutes.

The actual site or store creator engine is simple to use,

albeit a bit industrial. Most of the steps in the site builder wizard are text-driven and rely on pull-down menu type selection tools. The majority of the tools are found along a top navigation bar that resembles most Microsoft menus. There you'll find the icons that open up the modules for your site design, shipping options, product importing, and the like. What the system lacks in design template tools and options, it makes up in the shipping and and payment wizards that allow you to drop in a variety of customer choices.

Mycart charges no set-up fees, and their pricing package is as simple as their site navigation—$29.95 per month. If you like to compare, Mycart does some of the work for you, and provides a side-by-side, feature-by-feature chart pitting their biz-wiz builder against Yahoo! and others. Granted, the chart is skewed to favor Mycart, but it does give you a good starting point for your own evaluations.

Built in features such as a variable sales tax calculator, UPS shipment wizard, extensive search options, order notification by fax, e-mail, or even pager makes Mycart a must-see for those that have product sales at the core of their E-Business site.

	Cost	Tools	Designs	Look	Feel	Extras	OVERALL
Mycart	$	••••	•••	•••	•••	••••	••••

NetscapeVirtualOffice/Netopia E-Business
nvo.Netopia.com

The first impression you have regarding this relatively expensive set of E-Business building packages will be dependent on how you get to them. If you go by way of the Netscape-branded version first, you'll likely think a lot less of the programs than if you enter through the Netopia gate directly.

You'd think with whatever remaining brand equity Netscape has managed to hold on to over the years that they would be more particular about what they hang their name on. For reasons that are not explained anywhere on either site, the Netopia system that is offered on the public Netscape platform, dubbed the NVO, or Netscape Virtual Office, feels like an old motel room before the renovation.

I hate to think that the Netscape icon is being relegated to course that which old-fashioned brands usually follow, and like the Cartier logo on a cheap gym bag, is posted on sites that don't remotely represent the early Netscape culture. I can't speak to the way the site presents itself on AOL, but on my Internet Explorer browser, it was sort of a hodge-podge. For example, an interstitial pops up whenever you go to the homepage, advertising free domain name registrations if you can believe it, by calling an 800 number.

You then see two virtual chalk boards, with 8-point type describing the two packages. They seem to be trying to articulate every possible scenario here, and it's difficult to read through it all. If you jump to the FAQ section thinking it will be a more express journey to the facts, you'll find even more long, detailed text. The first clue you have that maybe they are trying too hard, or targeting someone other than you is when you see the first question in the FAQ: "What is a website?"

With rigid templates that are preloaded with sections that you can't change, and a relatively tame design and look, this system has the aura of an enterprise that is being maintained, rather than improved.

The prices advertised are Brochure, $19.95; Standard, $59.95; Super 200, $99.95; and Super 500, $149.95; per month each, but the Netopia annual fees are steep. You'll pay from $199 for the low-end, up to $1,499 at the high end, on top of the monthly fees.

What looks for all intents and purposes like the exact same set of packages and programs, but dressed up nicer and presented in a much more direct way, is the Netopia E-Business builder. Here you'll find the same deals, down to the exact package names as on the Netscape version, with a little more flair, and a hint that the end product might look pretty decent. If the annual fees mentioned above don't scare you away, this is worth investigating. There are two differences that I could find. Netopia is actively selling this ASP package to VARs, and there was a special on the Netscape version offering 13 months for the price of 12 at press time.

	Cost	Tools	Designs	Look	Feel	Extras	OVERALL
NVONetopia $$$		•••	•••	••	••	••	•••

NetStores by Fishbone Communications
NetStores.com

For those who like to evaluate systems by surveying existing customer sites, NetStores has scores of apparently satisfied customers and their sites available for your unlimited perusal. There are a wide variety of stores and storefronts featured, but a large percentage seem to be involved with publishing books and music.

The NetStores site building system is based on pre-built storefronts that you can then modify and customize using the usual assortment of options, but the end results break no new ground on layout or design. What really distinguishes NetStores from the rest is their pricing structure—very costly on the front end. The NetStores E-Commerce solution gives you an unlimited number of products, and the monthly fee is an affordable $50 per month. But the set-up fee for this baby is $595. NetStores Shopping Cart Transaction System, which is presented as the junior version of the above, also offers an unlimited number of products for $50 per month, but then there is an $80 per month virtual hosting fee, and a set up fee to start of $395. If you only want the NetStores Virtual Hosting package that simply provides 10Mb of storage and 1.5Gb transfer per month you'll pay a $150 set-up fee and $30 per month.

With copyrights on the site dating back as far as 1995, and scores of clients using the system, you'd think that NetStores would have built up a competitive advantage or brand distinction over some of the newer ASP biz-wiz builders, but there really isn't anything here about which to rave. For those who can get over or around the set-up fees, and like what NetStores did with "Wayne's Garage" or "Fulcrum Publishing," this may be of interest.

	Cost	Tools	Designs	Look	Feel	Extras	OVERALL
NetStores	$$$	•••	••	•••	•••	•	••

OhGolly
OhGolly.com

If you are looking for the express lane to E-Business development, visit OhGolly. With a 40-point headline that reads: "Design, build and manage a website for small business. Right here. Right now," and three numbered options that simply say, "Learn More," "Tour," and "Build Your Site," OhGolly will get you where you want to go, fast.

When you get there, you'll be pleasantly surprised at what you see. Creatively, OhGolly's templates and design elements stand out above the rest in those subtle kinds of ways that only artists understand completely, but that most people can recognize the moment they see it. They must be doing something right. According to OhGolly, since 1999, over 100,000 small businesses have taken advantage of their services.

Pricing levels are categorized as Good, Better, Even Better, and Best, and range from free (but you have advertising banners), to $29.95, $49.95, and $99.95, per month, for 100, 300, 500, and unlimited items, respectively. You get 5MB of space with the free package, then 50MB, 75MB and 100MB for the next up the scale. The only pricing details that might cause some to pause are the set up fees. There is no set-up fee at all for the free package, but at $299, $499, and $999, for the others, the OhGolly top end is higher than most. Granted, they do add a couple of nice extras if you go the stratosphere route.

At the "Best" level, you get 8 hours of help from your own "Customization Coach" to launch your site, and then one hour every month thereafter to help you make changes and modifications. There are other vapor-benefits like a coupon for a digital camera, and monthly search engine submissions, but ultimately your decision comes down to whether or not you want to pay extra to have some help. If $999 to start isn't completely prohibitive, there may be many who, after looking at the kind of professional product OhGolly and their coaches put out, will go for this higher-priced, higher-quality option. Here's how they stack up:

	Starter Site	Premier Biz	Premier Plus	Premier Pro
Catalog Items	100	300	500	unlimited
Total MB	5	50	75	100
Domain Hosting	Yes	Yes	Yes	Yes
Search Engine	One Time	Monthly	Monthly	Monthly
Ads Removed	No	Yes	Yes	Yes
Unique E-mail	No	Yes	Yes	Yes
Set-up Help	No	No	3 hours	8 hours
Help/month	No	No	No	1 hour
Set-up Cost	N/A	$299	$499	$999
Cost/mo.	N/A	$29.95	$49.95	$99.95
Cost/yr.	N/A	$299	$499	$999

	Cost	Tools	Designs	Look	Feel	Extras	OVERALL
OhGolly	$$	•••	••••	••••	•••	•••	••••

ShopCart
ShopCart.com

Starting with the ostentatious logo of a giant dollar sign in a shopping cart, and continuing with endless scrolling pages of text, this site building app has a lot to wade through before you get to the heart of their system. Unfortunately, once you do finally look at the demo and try their "1-2-3 Setup," things don't get any better.

For reasons not intuitively obvious to me, ShopCart goes to great lengths not only to show lines of HTML code that you'll need to "copy, paste, and modify" to build your site, but they talk about the code endlessly. Whether it's to downplay the difficulty, with phrases such as, "Just to let you know up front that it will be very easy to design your order pages using the programming listed below...honest," or to warn us with such statements as "you must insert 'add+' for the location of your order pages," the predominate theme is clearly "code." By the time I read the conclusion of a page suggesting I "review more online samples of codes...right now," I knew it was over. ShopCart lists pricing as $60 set-up fee, $35 per month.

Because in the broadest sense of the definition, this could still be classified as an instant app ASP model, and because there may be an adventuresome soul or two who want to dive into this cutting, pasting, and modifying HTML code scenario, we include ShopCart in our reviews. For the average organization, and most individuals, this would not be the logical first choice.

	Cost	Tools	Designs	Look	Feel	Extras	OVERALL
ShopCart	**$$**	•	•	••	•	•	•

Verio
Verio.com

Verio's entry in the instant E-Business app category leads off with a $24.95 "Express Start" package that is one of the quickest in the market. By simply clicking on the Express Start icon, you find yourself on the first build screen, choosing layout, colors, and the seven pages that are included with this package. Although the templates and design options are limited, for those that are looking to build and launch fast, there is probably no more efficient choice. You'll pay a $50 set-up fee, and get 10MB of space, and 1000MB of bandwidth/month.

Jumping to the merchant side, Verio boasts an E-Commerce building system that enables merchants to "point and click to build and securely operate a virtual storefront, and includes Web-site hosting, E-Commerce software, an online merchant account application, credit card processing, domain-name registration, and website traffic generation. No hidden fees or other vendors necessary: store building tool, merchant account, credit card processing gateway, secure hosting, and a listing in stuff.com all for one monthly fee."

They are promoting two versions. The Verio Store Builder, at $129.95/month plus a $100 set-up fee, includes up to 60MB of space, and can be completed in 15 minutes using their building "wizard."

The Verio Store Builder Pro, with up to 100MB of space, is $159.95/month with a $100 set-up fee. Both promote an unlimited number of products as part of their packages, but the fine print admits that the number is usually no more than 2000 items. They also have an alternative pricing page that shows packages for 300 items to run $199/month and up to 5000 items for $399/month.

That Verio is, at its core, the world's largest site hosting company is evident everywhere. It's sometimes hard to tell who is actually building and managing your site here. In one place you are using the "Shopsite" builder, yet the system is "Powered by Open Market," and affiliated with Lycos. The Verio homepage navigation isn't much help either, because Verio is still in the business of selling hosting, and most of the site is dedicated to that end.

The site builder itself offers a limited number of choices, and surprisingly, reveals some of the HTML coding and the programming language (that usually runs in the background of other systems) while you are in the process of designing and building. The end result is a simple four-step building wizard that looks a lot more complex that it is, and that produces a site that is a lot less interesting than you expect. For those who like one-stop shopping, with everything included in one package, Verio may provide the best option.

	Cost	Tools	Designs	Look	Feel	Extras	OVERALL
Verio	$	••••	•••	•••	••••	••••	••••

Vista
Vista.com

There is a refreshingly simple and upbeat user experience awaiting you at the Vista site, starting with their unique approach to getting you started on their site builder. Instead of asking you to fill out forms first, Vista asks only for your phone number, saying: "Vista has provided you with a head start. Your online business is waiting for you right now. Simply complete the information below, hit 'CONTINUE' and get started!" Granted, there is a short wizard to go through, but the effort seems minimal and the journey quick.

This is the kind of site you don't mind recommending to your friends, so well balanced the design and so customer-focused the approach. Admittedly, some of it is a little over the top, like quoting Jupiter's estimate that the average cost to have a Web development company create a commerce-enabled site and maintain it for one year ranges between $30,000 to $100,000. But as apologists for both their products, as well as the entire ASP industry, Vista makes the case well in word and deed.

You won't need to search very long for anything on the Vista site. The left hand navigation bar has a delightfully short list with three simple options: "Take the Tour," "See the Sites," and "Try it Now." While others offer an almost endless variety of packages and pricing models, Vista goes the other way, and like Southwest Airlines, offers a basic package that they deliver well at a great price/value. Real world client example sites are numerous, the tour is easy to navigate and understand, and all the tools are available for previewing, testing and even playing with. Thankfully, it is not text-heavy. Screen grabs and illustrations on a healthy dose of white space make Vista one of the most comfortable to use.

The site builder itself is empowered by a "Management Console," a comparatively tame icon-centric point-and-click design that is brilliant without being complex, and can deliver a nice range of design options and layout architecture. It is the extras that Vista added to the standard package that may be of interest to many, and sets them apart. The ability to easily add auctions, E-Commerce, community, appointment- and reservation-taking, weather updates, message boards, and store specials transforms average sites into real workhorses, which look and feel much more costly that they are.

Vista offers a 60-day free trial, and lists regular monthly fees at $49.95/month, but then immediately cuts that to $29.95/month, if you agree to 12 months in advance. At press time, even that was being discounted to only $19.95/month.

With free telephone-based online training, a Small Business Center loaded with tips, newsletters, and other resources, and a proactive approach to customer support and service, Vista demonstrates that though younger than most, they came to play and compete. For those who prefer the newest model on the road, or for any who are looking for an extremely fast and easy site-building experience that is a good value and presents your business in a high-quality way, Vista is definitely worth a test-drive.

	Cost	Tools	Designs	Look	Feel	Extras	OVERALL
Vista	$$	••••	••	••••	••••	•••••	••••

Wired-2-Shop by ET Technologies
Wired-2-Shop.com

The moment you arrive at what Wired-2-Shop calls "your only feature-rich store builder of choice," you know what their positioning strategy is—take the Yahoo! store builder and make it better. Whether they achieve that goal is largely dependent on whether or not you consider the added features valuable to your E-Business, but the good news is, they do part of the comparative work for you. A simple click on the "Product" page reveals a head-to-head comparison matrix that pits the Wired-2-Shop system against the Yahoo! version in the classic Coke vs Pepsi framework. There are over thirty listed features, and granted some of those that Wired-2-Shop includes, such as "ability to associate sounds," are probably not important to most of us. But other features, such as what they describe as "true drag and drop" design, and the ability to create your site in different languages, do stand out as significant differences.

Wired-2-Shop's builder interface will be a delight to those who are comfortable in the Microsoft world, and who want an extra level of customization in the size and scope of their site. With store element details that include the ability to vary taxes and currencies, and an almost infinite number of page layout configurations using easy drag-and-drop construction, this is one site-building system where the sky is really the limit.

They also work hard at making the pricing straightforward, even though the Canadian/US comparitors get a little laborious. The Micro-Store Package includes 50 items and has a CDN$50 (US$35) set-up charge and a CDN$60 (US$40) monthly fee. The Macro-Store is 250 items is CDN$80 to set-up and CDN$75/month. The Mega-Store ramps up to 1000 items with CDN$100 to set-up and a monthly rate of CDN$200.

Wired-2-Shop is not the cheapest model on the lot, especially for those who have more than 1,000 products, or for those who don't want to pay a premium for the extra non-essential features. As a shopping system that has built out a number of extra options and benefits for the business owner looking to do online commerce, it is definitely worth a test drive.

	Cost	Tools	Designs	Look	Feel	Extras	OVERALL
Wired-2-Shop $$		••••	••••	••••	••••	•••	••••

Yahoo! Site and Store
Site.Yahoo!.com   Store.Yahoo!.com

As mentioned at the top of this chapter, the Yahoo! Site building system is a slim but powerful little workhorse that is long on features and functionality, yet short on expense. More than one competitor openly admits using the Yahoo! Site as their model for their own biz-wiz system, and it's easy to see why.

It starts with the Yahoo! culture, and their resolute confidence in knowing what makes a winning E-Business site. Like other Yahoo! products, this is not the place to find the latest animation or streaming media technology. Yahoo! Site builder *will* give you the ability to have an easy-to-navigate, fast-loading, business-style site that caters to your customers. It will give you an above-average selection of template and design styles, but will not let you have complete control over all elements of the layout. It will allow the first-time user the ability to build and launch their site in real time, in less than five minutes, and it will also allow the experienced user to use more advanced tools. In short, the Yahoo! Site sets certain limits, in order to deliver better, consistent results.

This is also a system that charges a flat fee, period. It's $29.95/month for the basic site (25 MB of space, unlimited bandwidth, no set-up fees); $100/month for commerce. You can upgrade your site to commerce anytime you want, and grow into your E-Business development by moving to the Yahoo! Store option. Yahoo! Store uses the same tools and elements from your Yahoo! Site, and converts your system to online commerce seamlessly. It is used by more E-Businesses for online commerce than all of the competition combined, and shows products in the typically clean, uncluttered Yahoo! style.

With a slew of online reports and stats, an online reference manual, and a variety of ways to edit and modify your site in real time, the Yahoo! Site and Store are still tough to beat for the money. If you are looking for a way to build and launch an E-Business site or store with minimum hassle, minimum learning curve, yet still have room to grow and expand, this may be the best value in the market.

	Cost	Tools	Designs	Look	Feel	Extras	OVERALL
Yahoo!	$	●●●●	●●●●	●●●●	●●●●	●●●●	●●●●●

Zingstore
home.Zingstore.com

If Wired-2-Shop is a loaded convertible Thunderbird, then Zingstore is a stripped-down '68 Ford Galaxy. Nothing new or innovative here, although as a relatively new entrant, Zingstore may be still a work in progress. However, with a name that starts with "Zing," this site definitely needs to offer more in their E-Business building system to set it apart.

Zingstore is clearly focused narrowly on E-Commerce site building, and if that's all you are interested in, it may be worth a look. Their goal is to provide "a turnkey, E-Commerce solution that allows small and mid-size businesses a powerful and easy method to develop their e-business and strategy." Using their Web-based solution, Zingstores says their merchants can build a website and online catalog of products complete with a secure shopping cart and the Cardservice LinkPoint Gateway for secure online credit card processing.

If this Cardservice LinkPoint Gateway is important to you, then the Zingstore is a clear pathway there. Cardservice International is behind the site, and as a transaction service provider, is clearly hoping you'll use the Zingstore gateway into their services. Unfortunately, even their demo doesn't tell you what your cost will be, and when you ask for it, the dreaded "we'll get back to you" form is your only recourse.

	Cost	Tools	Designs	Look	Feel	Extras	OVERALL
Zingstore	$	●●	●●	●●	●		●

Zy
Zy.com

There are probably as many ways to present an E-Business builder as there are ways to name a product using obtuse two-letter combinations, but Zy is just eccentric enough to to stand out from the crowd. Picture a home page designed by Ray Walston in 1965 and you'll be in the right mindset. It's not just the presentation, though. The Zy package offers a number of features that no one else does.

The first thing you notice is the three-package approach. Zy captures a lot of attention with its ads for stunning webpages, free graphical headings, buttons, bullets, backgrounds, dividers, customized headings, button bars, java effects, photos, visitor counters, and banners. ZyWeb, the first package, is FREE, and includes up to 5 webpages, 10Mbytes of web storage, and webpage builder with 10 buttons, 10 headings, paragraph headings, backgrounds, dividers and bullets, choice of 40 Fonts, 5 banner ad styles to customize, unlimited photo storage and photo editor, free submission to 10 search engines and directories (option for 850+), visit counter on each page, e-mail address with mail forwarding and user support via online forums.

ZyPremium, the second package, is $7.95 per month unlimited access, or $79 per year, also unlimited access, which includes unlimited webpages, 20Mbytes of web storage, and a greater range of graphic designs and templates with 70 buttons, 80 headings, 12-3D spinning logos, 7 paragraph headings, 38 banners, 20 backgrounds, 60 dividers, 60 bullets, 150 fonts, 38 banner ad styles to customize, unlimited photo storage and photo editor, enhanced file store to store a wide range of file types, visit counter on each page, 5 e-mail addresses with mail forwarding, removable banner ads from the service pages, higher performance servers, data backed up for more security, create stand-alone graphics, free submission to 10 search engines and directories (option for 850+), discounted prices on advanced Search Engine Submission, use of own domain name (domain hosting fee applies), and priority e-mail support and online forums.

ZyBusiness, the third package, is $29.95 per month or $299 per year, unlimited access and includes free domain name of your choice—registration and hosting, unlimited webpages, 30Mbytes of web storage, license for commercial use, and greater range of graphic designs and templates with 70 buttons, 80 headings, 12-3D spinning logos, 7 paragraph headings, 38 banners, 20 backgrounds, 60 dividers, 60 bullets, 150 fonts, 38 banner ad styles to customize, unlimited photo storage and photo editor, enhanced file store to store a wide range of file types, visit counter on each page, 10 e-mail addresses with mail forwarding, removable banner ads from the service pages, create stand alone graphics, free submission to 10 search engines and directories (option for 850+), discounted prices on advanced search engine submission, faster performance servers, data backed up for more security, and priority e-mail support and user support, via online forums.

All the packages allow you to use Zy Modules for free, which is a nice touch considering they include some precoded Active Server Page and Java applets that you can paste right in to your site.

Zy is a clever, eccentrically brilliant biz-wiz system that offers something for everyone, and for the experience alone is worth checking out. When you add up all the tools and extras Zy offers, and compare it to their low pricing models, you may find this app on tap to be irresistible.

	Cost	Tools	Designs	Look	Feel	Extras	OVERALL
Zy	$	••••	•••••	•••••	••••	•••	•••••

Key To The Rating System

Cost- The monthly rental fee for the basic site or store as presented, including any extra fees to set-up or launch, but *not* including merchant fees or other transaction fees.

$	FREE - $29.99/month
$$	$30.00- $79.99/month
$$$	$80.00- $159.99/month
$$$$	$160.00-$249.99/month
$$$$$	>$250.00/month

Note: If a package is priced at $29.95/month but also requires a $100 set-up fee, we would amortize the $100 over 12 months and add the resultant $8.33 to the $29.95 to get an average monthly cost of $38.28—which would mean a cost code of "$$."

Tools- Quantity and quality of user-available site creation and builder tools available to the first-time or basic user. These are the mechanisms and the motors you'll use to build your E-Business.

•••••	Above-average quantity of tools that are fully intuitive, and deliver dramatic results
••••	Above-average quantity of tools that are easy to use, and deliver above-average results
•••	Average quantity of tools that are okay to use and deliver average results
••	Either below average quantity or below average quality of tools delivering average results
•	Below average tools that deliver below average results

Designs- The quantity and quality of templates, layouts, and other user-controllable variables such as colors, font sizing, elements, and placement frames to create maximum customization. These are the materials and supplies available to personalize your site.

- •••••   >100 templates or layout designs plus a wide variety of additional user-controlled variables
- ••••   > 75 templates or layout designs plus above average number of user-controlled variables
- •••   > 50 templates or layout designs with average number of user-controlled variables
- ••   > 20 templates or layout designs with limited number of additional user variables
- •   Less than 20 templates or layout designs with limited or no additional user variables

Look- How professional and high-quality the resultant site or store appears to the business user through the presentation of graphics, design, composition and elements. This is your site's or store's presentation to your customers.

- •••••   Best looking site and site elements throughout entirety of user's experience
- ••••   Above average looking site and site elements throughout entirety of user's experience
- •••   Average looking site throughout or parts of site inconsistent with others
- ••   Below average look in majority of pages
- •   Poor presentation throughout

Feel- Degree to which user finds easy, intuitive navigation, fast-loading pages, elements, and correct efficient operation throughout the site. This is how your E-Business runs.

- •••••   Excellent operation in every category
- ••••   Above average operation
- •••   Average operation
- ••   Below average operation
- •   Poor or non-functioning operation

Extras- Additional elements or features that provide unique or unusually valuable benefits.

●●●●●	Extras and benefits too numerous to count
●●●●	Lots of extras with many benefits
●●●	Significant extras and benefits
●●	Some extras or benefits
●	At least one extra that provides at least one unique benefit.

Overall- The average of all five categories *not including cost,* which stands alone. There could be, as a result, both a very low-cost and high-cost provider scoring the same. Or conversely, there could be three providers offering their services for less than $30.00/month, with only one scoring above-average overall. Use the categories individually to find those criteria that are most important to your E-Business, see which providers score highest, and then go directly to their sites to refine your decision and evaluate further.

N/D = Not Disclosed

Summary

There is no question that ASP-based site and store-building apps have established a firm foothold in the E-Business development marketplace, and will continue to be a leading solution for businesses and organizations of every size and budget. As of press time, Wall Street analysts were continuing to forecast tremendous growth for this sector, one of the new darlings of the investment community.[1] Biz-wiz systems like those reviewed herein will continue to evolve and improve, and new players will continue to appear in this explosive market. For additional information, fresh insights on the new players entering this market, and updates to all reviews, check out E-Business To Go online by going to: www.Appallaso.com and clicking on the E-Business To Go link, or go directly to E-BusinessToGo.com.

If you have discovered or are using a biz-wiz that you feel should be included in the next edition of E-Business To Go, please e-mail me directly at gLiam@E-BusinessToGo.com or through my publisher at AppallasoEditor@hotmail.com. Those that do so and supply their own review will receive an autographed copy of E-Business To Go, and if desired, will see their review posted on the E-Business To Go online site.

APPENDICES

Free Online Resources to Keep Your E-Business Knowledge Current

With the pace of the Connected Economy moving faster than even digital publishers can match, plugging into online knowledge banks or subscribing to online newsletters to stay current is as important as reading books like E-Business To Go. The following list represents a wide range of free online resources designed to inform and educate you about doing business in today's marketplace. While many are associated with, or sponsored by, a parent company or corporation that is in the business of making a profit, none restricts access to their resources, nor mandates payment of any kind. For additional sources, searching any of the popular engines using keywords such as "E-Business Resources" is guaranteed to bring up hundreds of results.

AllBusiness.com
www.Allbusiness.com
Free expert advice, dozens of free tools, plus thousands of Small Business service providers.

AMEX Small Business
www.AmericanExpress.com
Small Business planning tools, articles and experts are all designed to help you succeed.

Apple.com
www.apple.com
Whether or not you use Apple products, if you're a small business, this classy site loaded with tools, tips, and forums is for you.

BizProWeb.com

www.Bizproweb.com

Come here for comprehensive small business resources with how-to features, shareware, and discussion groups.

Bizzed

www.bizzed.com

Visit Citibank's site for news, tools and networking with significant content under each category.

Business Owner's Toolkit

www.Toolkit.cch.com

This free Toolkit has an insurance/finance feel, but the business tools, guidebooks and searchable how-to articles are current, and concise.

Business Resource Center

www.morebusiness.com

Skim their articles, how-to library, templates and online community.

Center for Advancement of Small Business

www.sbpm.gwu.edu/research/centers/CASB/electronic.htm

This large collection of resources with a scholarly approach will fascinate the intellectual mind.

E-Commerce.About.com

www.about.com

About.com includes free courses on E-Commerce 101, plus articles and searchable archives of discussion groups and forums.

ELab

www.E-Commerce.vanderbilt.edu

Since 1994, Vanderbilt has researched and examined E-Business, and this site has an almost unlimited backlog of that wisdom.

Entrepreneurial Edge
www.SmallBizNet.com
Deep website with libraries of over 4000 current and past "how to" articles make researching a less-daunting task.

Fambiz.com
www.Fambiz.com
Billed as the web's leading resource for family business executives and owners, the site has one of the fastest pathways to articles and other websites by topic.

Let's Talk Business
www.Ltbn.com
The "Let's Talk Business Network" site that has community and linking members at its core, also includes radio and other resources designed to help owners and managers succeed.

Microsoft bCentral
www.bcentral.com
The Small Biz needs to look no further for education, management and marketing tools.

Office.com
www.office.com
From online advertising and architecture to finding a web designer, this site's free content is some of the best in the business.

Quicken Small Business
www.quicken.com
True to form, Quicken offers Small business E-Business advice and management insights with a financial flavor.

SmallOffice.com
www.Smalloffice.com
This site gives reviews and recommendations on tools and techniques.

Smartbiz.com
www.smartbiz.com
Thousands of free resources including hundreds of free newsletters geared to the SMB an E-Business are right at your fingertips.

Yahoo! Small Business
www.Smallbusiness.yahoo!. com
Stock up on free tools, articles, and topics on E-Business and commerce in the typically no-fluff Yahoo! presentation.

Smart Ways to Find IT Solutions Providers

If you've determined that you need to find an IT generalist or specialist to help build or maintain your E-Business enterprises, there are a number of ways to search for the right provider. Getting a recommendation from a friend or peer whose E-Business system is similar to yours is always a good place to start, as is your city's local Business Journal (www.bizjournals.com). Another low-cost approach is to turn to the online exchanges, where you can draw from a national, or even international, pool of experts who can help guide you to the right organization for little, if any, cost up front. Here are a few that have deep resources:

CodeMarket.com
www.codemarket.com
Post your project needs for free, and hundreds of developers may bid on your job. You'll only pay a commission if there's a match.

Collab.net
www.collab.net
Thousands of IT developers in the Collab network are at your disposal. You pay a fee for their service.

Exp.com
www.exp.com
One of the largest online marketplaces, Exp.com links thousands of IT developers (experts) with projects you post online. If there is a match, the agreement includes paying a commission.

Expertcity.com
www.expertcity.com
With a realtime online expert, get help and pay by the question. The average you'll pay is $12 per inquiry, plus a 15% commission. It's a fast, affordable way to get quick answers.

ExpertsExchange.com
www.expertsexchange.com
Here's a free collaboration service that links IT professionals and companies.

HotDispatch.com
www.hotdispatch.com
Do you need a link to IT solutions providers? You can have free membership and pay a commission if a match is made.

ITRadar.com
www.itradar.com
Free to buyers, posts IT service providers' listings for around $75 each.

Itsquare.com
www.itsquare.com
Free to buyers, it charges a commission to IT service providers if the deal is made.

Openitx.com
www.openitx.com
Free online linkage and collaboration resource with a wide variety and range of expertise.

Questionexchange.com
www.questionexchange.com
Open exchange of question and answer posts where buyers and sellers set a price for the information, and then pay a small commission to the host.

E-Business Agencies and Firms
With a Range of Services

The companies listed herein have capabilities in a variety of areas of E-Business, from strategic planning to site architecture, design, implementation and e-marketing, and may be a resource to assist with all or part of an E-Business development. Those shown below have indicated a willingness to work with companies of all sizes and are not exclusively focused on big business; however, all E-Agencies should be evaluated not only for a capabilities and budget match, but size and culture as well. The listings that follow represent a wide range of firm size and experience levels and are shown in alphabetical order. Inclusion in this list does not constitute any endorsement by the author.

Agency.com
665 Broadway, New York, NY 10012
Phone 212-358-8220 Fax 212-358-8255
www.agency.com

Anne Holmes and Associates
5117 Jersey Ridge Rd., Davenport, IA 52807-3134
Phone 319-344-9434 Fax 319-344-9386
www.anneholmes.com

BAM
152 Notre Dame Est., #200, Montreal, Quebec H2Y 3P6
Phone 514-875-1500 Fax 514-875-2108
www.bam.net

Banta Integrated Media
222 Third Street, Cambridge, MA 02142
Phone 617-497-6811 Fax 617-441-9265
www.banta-im.com

Big Theory
2216 Commerce St., Dallas, TX 75201
Phone 214-748-5901 Fax 214-748-6431
www.bigtheory.com

Blast Radius
594 Broadway, Suite 206, New York, NY 10012
Phone 212-925-4900 Fax 212-925-5247
www.blastradius.com

Blue Dingo
665 Broadway, 6th Fl., New York, NY 10012
Phone 212-358-8080 Fax 212-358-8085
www.bluedingo.com

Breakaway Solutions
50 Rowes Wharf, Boston, MA 02110
Phone 617-960-3400 Fax 617-960-3434
www.breakaway.com

Brighton Interactive
25 N. Brentwood, St. Louis, MO 63105
Phone 314-725-8025 Fax 314-725-8001
www.brightoninteractive.com

Carton Donofrio Interactive
120 W. Fayette St., Baltimore, MD 21201
Phone 410-576-9000 Fax 410-752-2191
www.cdinteractive

CE Communications/tdah! Digital Solutions
30400 Van Dyke Avenue, Warren, MI 48093
Phone 810-558-7043 Fax 810-558-5821
www.cecom.com

Clear Ink
3000 Oak Road, Walnut Creek, CA 94596
Phone 925-937-2100 Fax 925-817-8400
www.clearink.com

Click Here
7007 Twin Hills, Dallas, TX 75231
Phone 214-378-3112 Fax 214-378-3101
www.clickhere.com

Collaborate
445 Bush St., San Francisco, CA 94108
Phone 415-651-1200 Fax 415-206-1720
www.collaborate.com

Corporate Graphics
76 Otis Street, Westboro, MA 01581
Phone (508) 898-2500 Fax (508) 898-2691
www.corporategraphics.com

Cyber Sight
220 NW 2nd Ave., Portland, OR 97209
Phone 503-228-4008 Fax 503-228-3629
www.cybersight.com

Darwin Digital
375 Hudson Street, New York, NY 10014
Phone 212-807-3700 Fax 212-807-3725
www.darwindigital.com

DRG Interactive
266 Summer St., Boston, MA 02210
Phone 617-250-5000 Fax 617-250-5001
www.directresults.com

Emerging Media
633 Battery St., Suite 118, San Francisco, CA 94111
Phone 415-591-0400 Fax 415-591-0401
www.emergingmedia.com

Eye Dezine
22 Marbella, Irvine, CA 92614
Phone 949-752-1696 Fax 703-997-5993
www.eyedezine.com

Four Points Digital
400 W. Erie, #400, Chicago, IL 60610
Phone 312-280-2470 Fax 312-280-2680
www.four-points.com

Free Range Media
100 South King St., #600, Seattle, WA 98104
Phone 206-695-5700 Fax 206-695-5703
www.freerange.com

Fusive
800 Fairway Dr., Ste 100, Deerfield Beach, FL 33441
Phone 954-422-8300 Fax 954-571-3700
www.fusive.com

Giant Step
427 S. LaSalle, 6th Fl., Chicago, IL 60605
Phone 312-385-3000 Fax 312-385-3001
www.giantstep.com

Graphics & Motion
3125 S. Mendenhall Rd, Ste 312, Memphis, TN 38115
Phone 901-795-1387 Fax 901-795-0511
www.gmotion.com

Grey Interactive
111 Fifth Avenue, 2nd Floor, New York, NY 10003
Phone 212-420-5100 Fax 212-420-5151
www.greyinteractive.com

Harpell/Martins
12 Clock Tower Pl., Maynard, MA 01754
Phone 978-461-0202 Fax 978-461-0210
www.harpell.com

iAgency
2701 Ocean Park Blvd., #201, Santa Monica, CA 90405
Phone 310-664-6710 Fax 310-664-6711
www.iagency.com

Imaginet
2100 Metro Ctr, 333 S. 7th St., Minneapolis, MN 55402
Phone 651-704-6300 Fax 651-704-7733
www.imaginet.com

Imagio Technology Advertising and PR
316 Occidental Ave. So., #400, Seattle, WA 98104
Phone 206-625-0252 Fax 206-625-0271
www.imagio.com

ImC2
7505 John Carpenter Frwy, Dallas, TX 75247
Phone 214-224-1000 Fax 214-224-1100
www.imc2.com

Interactive Papyrus
30 E. Kiowa, Colorado Springs, CO 80903
Phone 719-633-7792 Fax 719-636-1886
www.ipapyrus.com

Internet One
1661 International Place, Suite 400, Memphis, TN 38120
Phone 901-888-2932 Fax 901-795-0511
www.Internetone.net

K2 Design
30 Broad Street, New York, NY 10004
Phone 212-301-8800 Fax 212-301-8801
www.k2design.com

Key Mind
6066 Leesburg Pike, Suite 200, Falls Church, VA 22041
Phone 703-578-1100 Fax 703-578-3200
www.keymind.com

Kingswood Interactive
Cricket Terrace Center, Ardmore, PA 19003
Phone 610-896-4620 Fax 610-896-9242
www.kingswood.com

Lowe Lintas Interactive
One Dag Hammarskjold Plaza, New York, NY 10017
Phone 212-605-8063 Fax 212-605-4714
www.lliny.com

Lucid Marketing
24 Tynemouth Court, Robbinsville, NJ 08691
Phone 609-426-1398 Fax 609-426-1584
www.lucidmarketing.com

Magnet
3255 Grace Street NW, Washington, DC 20007
Phone 202-625-1111 Fax 202-625-1342
www.magnet.com

MarchFirst
2880 Lakeside Dr., #300, Santa Clara, CA 95054
Phone 408-987-3200 Fax 408-987-3230
www.marchfirst.com

Max Commerce
1005 Aldeman Dr., #102 & #103, Alpharetta, GA 30005
Phone 770-442-3375 Fax 770-442-2272
www.maxcommerce.com

Net Performance
300 First Ave S., Suite 500, St. Petersburg, FL 33702
Phone 888-813-8133 Fax 727-524-8544
www.netperformance.com

Next Digital
2907 Bay to Bay Blvd., Tampa, FL 33629
Phone 800-923-8111 Fax 813-835-8812
www.nextdigital.com

Non Linear
168 Dalhousie Street, Ottawa, Ontario K1N 7C5
Phone 613-241-2069 Fax 613-241-3086
www.nonlinear.ca

Nyd2
217 Halls Mill Road, Lebanon, NJ 08833
Phone 908-534-6780 Fax 908-534-5374
www.nyd2.com

Ogilvy One
309 W. 49th Street, New York, NY 10019
Phone 212-237-6000 Fax 212-237-5123
www.ogilvy.com

Peec
491 Old York Rd., Suite 201, Jenkintown, PA 19046
Phone 215-881-9560 Fax 215-881-9562
www.peec.com

Quantum Leap Communications
22 W. Hubbard St., Chicago, IL 60610
Phone 312-494-0300 Fax 312-494-0120
Quantum.leapnet.com

Rabid Web
82 W. Del Amo Blvd., Long Beach, CA 90805
Phone 562-428-4493 Fax 562-428-4493
www.rabidweb.com

Razorfish
32 Mercer Street, New York, NY 10013
Phone 212-966-5960 Fax 212-966-6915
www.razorfish.com

Red Ant Media Group
5514 Wilshire Blvd., 8th Fl., Los Angeles, CA 90036
Phone 323-938-1211 Fax 323-938-0110
www.redant.net

Red Sky Interactive
921 Front St., San Francisco, CA 94111
Phone 415-392-2500 Fax 415-392-2501
www.redsky.com

Ribit Productions
14951 N. Dallas Parkway, #220, Dallas, TX 75240
Phone 972-239-8866 Fax 972-239-8788
www.ribit.com

Sapient
One Memorial Drive, Cambridge, MA 02142
Phone 617-621-0200 Fax 617-621-1300
www.sapient.com

Shandwick Interactive
8400 Normandale Lk Blvd., #500, Minneapolis, MN 55437
Phone 612-832-5000 Fax 612-831-9191
www.shandwick-interactive.com

Site Lab
2223 Avenida de la Playa, #208, La Jolla, CA 92037
Phone 619-456-4720 Fax 619-456-4724
www.sitelab.com

THINK New Ideas
45 West 36th St., New York, NY 10018
Phone 212-629-6800 Fax 212-629-6850
www.thinkinc.com

Thunderhouse Marketing Communications
56 West 22nd St., 12th Fl., New York, NY 10010
Phone 212-206-2700 Fax 212-206-2737
www.thunderhouse.com

US Interactive
28 West 23rd St., 12 Fl., New York, NY 10010
Phone 212-620-4040 Fax 212-620-7895
www.usinteractive.com

Viant
600 West Peachtree Street, Ste. 2300, Atlanta, GA 30308
Phone 404-260-1100 Fax 404-260-1101
www.viant.com

Website Dynamics
4211 Signal Rdg Rd. N.E., #2879, Cedar Rapids, IA 52406
Phone 319-395-6533 Fax 319-395-6575
www.websitedynamics.com

E-Business Online Publications

Some of the best print periodicals in the industry provide part, or in some cases all, of their paid-subscription magazine content online at no charge. The best "big six" are noted with an asterisk, but all of the following are reliable resources that should be part and parcel of every E-Business manager's online library.

*Business 2.0
www.Business2.com
The companion site to the award-winning print publication that was there from the beginning, this resource can be bookmarked as a one-stop gateway to hundreds of other industry resources. One of the big six, with some of the best writers and minds in the industry, a can't miss site.

Bloomberg Technology News
www.Bloomberg.com Investor oriented, still a one-stop shop for searchable inside information on any technology subject, trend, or challenge that could affect E-Business. Plus, the live news reports that stream all day long are always interesting.

Business Week E-Biz
www.Businessweek.com
Both the online version of the magazine and the separate E-Biz magazine site are worth the price of admission, and provide so many consistently insightful articles and resources for doing business in today's economy that you'll come back week after week.

CIO.com
www.cio.com
News, analysis, searchable archive, and a super learning reservoir in the WebBusiness section.

ClickZ Network

www.ClickZ.com

If you don't mind the sponsored content and occasional sales pitches from affiliates, you'll find major insights and current case studies on everything from e-mail marketing to stats, many of which are subscribable to be delivered to your e-mailbox free. Good on all permission-based, one-to-one subjects.

CMP's Information Week

www.Informationweek.com

This should be on everyone's list for some of the best breaking news, insights and analysis in the greater IT industry.

CMP's Internet Week

www.Internetwk.com

Explore this site for in-depth breaking news with specific focus on the Internet and E-Business.

CNNTechnology

www.CNN.com/TECH

Although CNN offers a more macro view of technology in general with a consumer slant, it still provides killer content with depth.

Cyber Atlas

www.Cyberatlas.Internet.com

Stats, demographics, snapshots, and more make this a site you'll fly through relatively quickly, but refer to often.

*E-Commerce Times

www.Ecommercetimes.com

It's international, rich, updated with the latest news every five minutes, (really), and it's irresistible. Use this as a gate to the NewsFactors and other great online resources.

eMarketer News
www.Emarketer.com
Register for daily news, stats, and e-intelligence, online directly, or delivered as newsbytes to your e-mail.

*Fast Company
www. Fastcompany.com
Another one of the big six, always current, decidedly fresh, yet consistently visionary sites. For fleshed out stories that are universally applicable to all E-Businesses, plus great community resources, put this site at the top of your list. Then, if you decide you want to subscribe to at least one E-publication, give serious consideration to this magazine.

Forbes Digital Tool
www.Forbes.com
What can you say about an icon that keeps changing with the times? Whatever Steve didn't spend running for President, he's clearly put into this product, and you can be sure to find information you can use.

Fortune's e-Company
www.Fortune.com
Here you'll find resources for all of your E-Business with small business resources, plus free newsletters and stories with a high-tech edge.

*Industry Standard
www.Thestandard.com
This is one of the big six that is a mandate for anyone doing business today—the 60-Minutes of our industry. If there was only one online publication you had time to take in each week, The Standard would have to be your choice.

*Internet.com
www.Internet.com
As the gateway to over a dozen channels of specific interest, you may select the E-Commerce channel for news, tools, marketing insights newsletters, and much more.

Red Herring
www.Redherring.com
Featuring the leading edge of technology news and analysis for investors and VCs, Red Herring's online publication is also loaded with enough trend-setting insight to keep your heart pumping. Be sure to hit the Inside Tech section.

Small Business Computing/Home Office Computing
www.DestinationSOHO.com
Two super magazines under one URL. When technology is the focus, many SMB and SOHO readers turn to Small Business Computing or its sister publication Home Office Computing as a first resource for insight, product reviews, and the latest news. You can have access to the same resources at no charge by going to this site.

Upside Today: The Tech Insider
www.Upside.com
Another gathering place for investors looking for tech trends, Upside online has just as much to offer the average business or organization scanning the horizon for the latest trends. With an E-Biz section and an E-Services module, Upside's online offering is a fast way to get current.

*ZDNet
www.Zdnet.com/Smallbusiness and
www.Zdnet.com/E-Commerce
The advice and reviews alone vault this early online leader to the top of the pack, but you'll make it your friend the moment you use the ZDNet search engine to search all the ZDNet resources for E-Business and Internet terms or technologies. It's one of the first places to turn to when you want lots of information on a subject fast.

* Indicates one of the "big six" stalwarts that I consider a mainstay of my E-Business resource pool.

GLOSSARY

Account Authority Digital Signature (AADS)--A payment mechanism combining smart cards and pin codes to create a unique digital signature for an online transaction.

Acrobat--(aka PDF); Adobe's popular document reader used as an easy, usually no-cost way to download documents from online sources.

ActiveX—A Microsoft software package and program that allows for including applications into HTML code.

ADSL—See Asymmetric Digital Subscriber Line.

Anonymous FTP—Ability to access computer without log-in or ID.

Applet—A "small application." This is generally a generic term for an ActiveX, Java or JavaScript type program. Some ASPs give users pre-written applets that can be simply selected, pasted and used.

Application—A program or piece of software designed to meet a specific purpose.

Application Service Provider (ASP)—A server-centric depository of applications (including software programs, online services, tools and templates) that are made available to online users through the Internet, usually at a significant reduction in cost. By allowing many users to "rent" the software and programs on an as-needed or on-demand basis, the cost is shared by many more users and essentially amortized across a larger pool for a fractional portion of the cost each. Site-building and store-building "biz-wiz" or "apps on tap" are just one type of ASP.

ARPANET—The original ancestor of the Internet, funded by the US Department of Defense.

ASP—See Application Service Provider.

ASP Pages—Microsoft-driven software that allows server-based scripts to generate dynamic web pages that load variable content.

Asymmetric Digital Subscriber Line (ADSL)—Fatter pipes that deliver faster data, using existing copper wires into locations served by standard telephone lines.

Attachment—A computer file that is electronically stapled to an e-mail message and sent with it.

Authorization—The approval given to credit card payment requests when the merchant account is valid, the credit card details provided are valid and the credit card has sufficient funds/credit available to complete the purchase.

B2B—See Business to Business.

B2C—See Business to Consumer.

Bandwidth—The amount of data that can be transmitted in a fixed amount of time. For digital devices, the bandwidth is usually expressed in bits or bytes per second (bps). For analog devices, the bandwidth is expressed in cycles per second, or Hertz (Hz).

BBS—See Bulletin Board System.

Bit—The smallest unit of measure for computer data. A bit can be on or off (a one or a zero) while strings of bits in various combinations are used to represent everything from music to spreadsheets and full-length movies.

Bitmap—A type of image created and displayed by aggregating dots. (See GIF and JPEG).

Boolean Search—A search engine directive that allows the searcher to include or exclude results or listings through the use of such modifiers as "AND," "NOT," and "OR."

Browser—The interface used to access the web, such as Microsoft's Internet Explorer or Netscape.

Bulletin Board System (BBS)—Early electronic message system that allowed users to dial up to read and post messages.

Business to Business (B2B)—A generic term used for any web application that is used by businesses to trade together. For example, an E-Business that provides sales personnel with online CRM or procurement.

Business to Consumer (B2C)—A generic term used for any web application that is used by businesses to sell directly to consumers (for example an E-Business selling perfume).

Byte—A group of eight bits. Computer memory is usually measured in bytes.

Cache—The high-speed storage mechanism that allows pages to load faster by holding data in either a reserved   section of main memory or an independent high-speed   storage device. Two types of caching are commonly used in personal computers: memory caching and disk caching.

CAD—See Computer-Aided Design.

CBT—See Computer-Based Training.

Chat—Online destinations where numerous visitors can discuss and communicate with each other in real time.

Chief Information Officer (CIO)—Officer or manager of an organization usually responsible for E-Business, Internet, Intranet, and Extranet enterprises.

Chief Knowledge Officer (CKO)—Officer or manager of an organization responsible for training team members.

CIO—See Chief Information Officer.

CKO—See Chief Knowledge Officer.

Client—Term for the computer that uses the services of another computer, or server.

Client/Server System—The protocol and procedure that has allowed the Internet in general, and ASPs specifically, to provide applications and services to numerous users simultaneously, anywhere in the world, 24/7.

Collaborative Software—Term for software that allows the sharing of resources, files and offer services to make working in an group easier.

Commerce Server—A server whose primary purpose is electronic commerce, including the presentation of products for sale, (online catalog) the actual ordering and payments process, (shopping cart) and tracking of shipments.

Computer-Aided Design (CAD)—Refers to any computer-enabled method of design; also called computer-assisted design.

Computer-Based Training (CBT)—Learning enterprises and training delivered through computers; typically refers to everything except Internet-based training. (See IBT.)

Configurator—Online product or service-building program that allows users to change components, ingredients or other variables and instantaneously see resultant configurations displayed. Can include a wealth of data, including pricing information, part numbers, and ordering capability. Configurators have been consistently rated by users as one of the top tools on the Internet, and by companies that provide configurators one of the top cost-savings modules of their E-Business enterprises.

Cookie—A small ID packet of information stored on end user's computers when the user visits a web site, to make online interaction more efficient. The cookie is "deposited" by the site onto the user's computer, and is used to hold session identifiers, preferences, or repeat information like a user's name, address and shopping preferences.

Database—A storage system for collecting, collating, and recalling data. In their most basic form, the Internet and E-Businesses are simply new ways of presenting variables from databases that are linked together and interact.

Data-Mining—The process of discovering previously unknown or untapped information from the data in data warehouses. For example, going back to site visitor reports and noting customer behavior, or tendencies.

Data Warehouse—A location where business knowledge and information are stored. Years ago, in shoe boxes. Today, usually on hard drives and servers.

DNS—See Domain Name Server.

Domain—Part of the official name of a computer on the Net. Domain names are unique identifiers, and can be secured through online registration services for periods of 1 year or more.

Domain Name Server (DNS)—The online server that translates between Internet domain names, such as E-BusinessToGo.com and Internet numerical addresses, such as 230.24.56.144

Download—Process of copying a file, document or application from one computer or resource to another.

E-Business—Any organization or individual engaged in the exchange of any goods, services, resources, ideas or things through the facility of the Connected Economy. E-Business includes but is not limited to E-Commerce, (where goods and services are exchanged or transacted for some tangible value), and encompasses the widest spectrum of activities brought about through the power of the connected marketplace.

E-Commerce—Originally limited to those business transactions conducted over the Internet where goods were exchanged for payments in cash, credit or debit. Today, more broadly refers to any online exchanges of value, whether they be in the form of money, tangible goods, credits, points, time, or other quantitative value exchange items.

EDI—See Electronic Data Interchange.

EFTPOS—See Electronic Funds Transfer at Point Of Sale.

Electronic Data Interchange (EDI)—The historic, pre-Internet electronic system deployed for the procurement of goods in the retail and manufacturing industries. EDI was the original business to business E-Commerce solution, still in use today and growing even better through online integration.

Electronic Funds Transfer at Point Of Sale (EFTPOS)—A payments mechanism that allows physical retailers to reliably process credit card transactions from their stores.

E-mail—The fast, efficient, and low-cost digital communications system that enables those online to send messages, files, documents and more to any other user or groups of users online through the facility of the Internet's connectivity.

Encryption—The recoding or scrambling technique that ensures that digital data is stored or transmitted in a way that makes it difficult for unauthorized third parties to have access to the original data.

Enterprise Resource Planning (ERP)—An integrated system of operation applications combining logistics, production, distribution, contract and order management, sales forecasting, customer, financial and HR management.

ERP—See Enterprise Resource Planning.

Extensible Hypertext Markup Language (XHTML)—An adaptation of XML that makes it easier to convert existing HTML web pages into a format understood by XML enabled web browsers.

Extensible Markup Language (XML)—A language for the Internet that provides additional functions beyond HTML. For example, while an HTML based web page will display pricing and product code information in a catalog site as text, XML can call up variable pricing or descriptions based on individual customers using the catalog at the time, or for different currencies from around the globe.

Extranet—An exclusive, usually gated intranet, extended outside the user location to others. Based on Internet standard protocols which allows access to the intranet, via the Internet, by people outside the enterprise, extranets are growing rapidly as a popular way to serve customers and employees with exclusive online privileges.

File Transfer Protocol (FTP)—A method of transferring files from one computer to another over the net.

Firewall—A gate or series of gates designed to restrict unauthorized or undesired access or input from outside the organization. Typically found in government and military sectors, many corporations have set up firewalls to keep competitors, viruses, and dirt out of their systems.

FTP—See File Transfer Protocol.

FTP Server—A computer on the Internet that stores files for transmission by FTP.

Gateway—A computer that connects one network with another, where the two networks use different protocols.

GIF—See Graphic Interchange Format.

Gigabyte—1,000,000,000, bytes or characters of data.

Graphic Interchange Format (.gif File)—A common file format for graphic images on the Internet. (See also JPEG and Bitmap).

Graphic User Interface (GUI)—The onscreen presentation of information in graphic or picture form, invented by XEROX and nurtured by Apple and Microsoft, that is standard for today's computers. Until GUI, computer users saw and interacted only with text on the screen.

GUI—See Graphic User Interface.

Handheld Device Markup Language (HDML)—One of the second-generation languages birthed from the Internet and HTML, designed to deliver content to handheld, portable, or other small access devices like PDAs or cellphones.

Hardware—The magnetic, mechanical and electrical components of a computer and its peripheral devices.

HDML—See Handheld Device Markup Language.

Header—The top of a webpage; or, the beginning of an e-mail message containing to and from addresses, subject, date, and other codes important to the programs that handle your mail.

Home Page—Originally used to describe a website, more commonly used to describe the first landing page a visitor goes to after loading in a URL address.

Host—A computer on the Internet.

Hostname—The name of the computer on the Internet.

HTML—See HyperText Mark-up Language.

HTTP—See HyperText Transfer Protocol.

HyperText Transfer Protocol (HTTP)—A variant of HTML that encrypts messages for security. The way in which the World Wide Web is transferred over the net.

HyperText Mark-up Language (HTML)—The first-generation language used on the World Wide Web. This language lets the text include both viewable text, and hidden codes that define fonts, layout, embedded graphics and hypertext links. This allows the seamless integration of different media and styles on one page.

IBT—See Internet-Based Training.

IEEE 1394—A serial protocol that runs at speeds ranging from 100 to 400 megabits per second, depending upon the implementation. Devices that are prime candidates for IEEE 1394 include digital camcorders and VCRs, digital audio amplifiers, and video teleconferencing.

Image—Technically, the computerized representation of a picture or graphic. More generally, any presentation on the screen other than text.

Image Resolution—The fineness or coarseness of an image as it is digitized; measured in dots per inch (DPI). The higher the DPI, the more precise the image, the more likely the image can be enlarged without pixelization or image loss, and the more time the image will usually take to load.

Information mapping—The process of locating important information and knowledge in an organization, then publishing a list or diagram showing where to find it.

Information Systems (IS) Strategy—The identification and prioritization of systems and applications for development.

Information Technology (IT)—A collective term used to refer to broadest definition of the hardware and software that is used to process information. In the 1980's IT departments handled "the computers." Today, IT is usually found everywhere in an organization.

Infotainment—One of the new connected economy terms used to describe the products that result from the convergence of information and entertainment.

Intangible Asset—A non-physical asset, such as a patent, a brand name or goodwill; it also encompasses the know-how embodied in employees or working practices.

Integrated Services Digital Network (ISDN)—A fast digital phone service that predated DSL, ADSL, cable et. al. and operates at speeds of up to 128 kilobytes per second.

Internet-Based Training (IBT)—Also referred to as web-based training. Exploded in popularity in late 1999 with ASP-based models like Click2Learn.com and TrainingDepartment.com.

Internet Explorer—One of the most popular web browser systems.

InterNIC—The original Internet Network Information Center, a central repository of information about the Internet itself.

Intranet—A private online network within an organization, gated (requiring ID and passcodes), usually protected from Internet traffic by a "firewall." Examples include online HR departments, online employee training modules, and online sales meetings.

ISDN—See Integrated Services Digital Network.

IT—See Information Technology.

IT Productivity Paradox—The often perplexing realization that what companies spend on technology to improve productivity in order to reduce costs, often ends up not being realized on the other end in practice due to offsetting increases in the costs to maintain and improve the technology.

Java—An Internet language invented by Sun Microsystems, often used to animate or provide interactivity online.

Joint Photographic Experts Group (JPEG)—Popular file format for images on the Internet ideal for photos and graphics with gradations in tone. A common form used by image and stock photo sources.

JPEG—See Joint Photographic Experts Group.

Kilobyte—One thousand bytes or characters of data.

Link—A Hypertext connection that when selected, takes users to another document or another part of the same document.

Lotus Notes—Software that pre-dated the Internet and allowed users to share a variety of information from a wide range of sources. Some early adopters used Lotus-Notes as their software of choice to launch first E-Business sites and systems.

Mail Server—The computer system/server on the Internet that provides mail services.

Mainframe—The central processing unit of a large computer, usually receiving input from a number of terminals.

Megabyte—One million bytes or characters of data.

Microprocessors—The tiny but powerful electronic circuitry that comprise a computer's central information processing unit.

Merchant Account—A bank account opened by a merchant with a bank or card issuer that allows the merchant to accept various forms of payment, usually a credit or debit card. Typically a merchant will require a single merchant account with their bank to accept Visa, MasterCard etc. Today merchant accounts are available from online providers that help minimize the cost and time that used to be required for set up, and which are designed for E-Business use exclusively.

Merchant Fee—The fee charged by the card issuers to allow businesses to take credit cards as payment, while the bank and card issuers take a measure of risk. The fee is negotiated with each merchant and ranges widely depending on the merchant's risk profile and value to the card issuer, but most fees for physical stores are between 2.5% and 5% of transaction value. Web based merchants may also have to pay an additional fee, on a fee per transaction or percentage of transaction value basis if they use a payments gateway service.

Micropayment—The facility to allow for small billables. Because some online transactions are not worth billing individually, (charging a nickel fee to view a news report, paying a web-referral of a penny per visitor), these fees are bundled until such time that value exceeds the processing cost of the transactions.

Modem—The inbound/outbound communications switch port that allows your computer to connect and talk to others through phonelines, cable, or other wired or wireless connectivity.

MPEG—See Motion Picture Experts Group.

Motion Picture Experts Group (MPEG)—One of two popular video file compression systems that condenses the large amounts of information necessary to store a video on a computer into a more manageable sized file.

Navigation—The set of buttons, links, or tabs found on an Internet site or E-Business system that allow the user to go to all the pages of the site. Often locked into a certain place on the screen, (left-hand navigation, for example) and made to be accessible consistently throughout the site, the navigation is one of the key ingredients to successful visitor experiences.

Netscape—One of the earliest and most popular web browsers. Networks: simply put, two or more computers connected together. Those in the same or nearby buildings are called local area networks (LAN); those that are connected over greater distances are called WANs, wide area networks. In a sense, the Internet and the global Connected Marketplace is a giant WAN.

Node—A computer on the net also called the host.

One-To-One—The marketing communications term for interacting with customers on individual, personalized levels where each person's name, preferences and desires are not only known, but also always part of the mix. Opposite of mass marketing.

Page—A screen, document or collection of information, available on the Internet, which may be communicated through any combination of various media, e.g., text, video, sound, interactive forms, etc.

PC—See Personal Computer.

PC Card—A popular methodology for expanding the capabilities of a PC or laptop, trademarked by PCMCIA. A removable device that is designed to be plugged into a PCMCIA slot and used as a memory-related peripheral.

PCI—See Peripheral Component Interconnect.

PCM—See Pulse Coded Modulation.

PCMCIA—See Personal Computer Memory Card International Association.

PDF File—One of the most popular methods for distributing formatted documents over the Internet. Users utilize the Acrobat 'reader' to see and control a digital document.

Peripheral Component Interconnect (PCI)—A high performance, 32-bit or 64-bit bus designed to be used with devices that have high bandwidth requirements, such as the display subsystem.

Personal Computer (PC)—Before or around 1984, it meant 'not IBM,' then 'not Macintosh.' Now it refers to any computer, Internet application appliance, or even peer-to-peer unit that you don't wear or carry in your pocket.

Personal Computer Memory Card International Association (PCMCIA)—Sometimes used to refer to a controller for a type of expansion card documented in the PCMCIA standards.

Ping—Similar to a sonar chirp, this is a program that checks to see whether you can communicate with another computer on the

Internet. It sends a short message to which the other computer automatically responds.

Pixels—An abbreviation for picture element. The minimum raster display element, represented as a point, with a specified color or intensity level. One way to measure picture resolution is by the number of pixels used to create images.

Plug-In—A computer program to add a Web browser that helps handle special file types (e.g. Flash Graphics).

Point of Presence (POP)—Large, hub-level full time links direct to the Internet, usually owned by Internet service providers or large companies due to the expense. Individuals will dial in through telephone lines or connect through an intranet to a POP server in order to access the Internet.

POP—See Point of Presence.

Post Office Protocol—A system by which a mail server on the Internet lets you pick up your mail and download onto your PC.

Program—The code behind the activity. A set of digitally coded definitions and instructions that enable a computer to perform a particular task. For example, Microsoft Word, Quark, and Excel. ASPs that provide "applications" (i.e. Application Service Providers) are essentially renting programs which are accessed and used on their servers.

Protocol—The language that one computer uses to communicate with another and the rules upon which the computers agree and rely to talk between themselves.

Pulse Coded Modulation (PCM)—A method of encoding information in a signal by varying the amplitude of pulses. The most common method of encoding an analog signal into a digital bit stream.

QuickTime—A video viewing program that allows full-motion video to be decompressed and streamed for viewing.

Real—Originally an audio, now a full media streaming program.

Router—A computer that connects two or more networks.

Secure Sockets Layer (SSL)—A security protocol first developed by Netscape that provides secure communication between a client's web browser and a web server, that prevents unauthorized users from accessing or seeing sensitive information like passwords or credit card details when transmitted over the Internet.

Serial Port—The plug to which the modem is connected.

Server—A computer that provides a service to other computers.

Shockwave—Program by Macromedia for animation and multimedia online.

Shopping Cart—The metaphorical online basket used by online shoppers to temporarily hold any items selected by customers at a web site before payment. At the conclusion of the purchasing process, consumers can review their selected items along with total purchase and shipping costs, and "check out." Most E-Commerce sites, and many ASP store builders give users shopping carts.

Simple Mail Transfer Protocol (SMUT)—The misnamed method by which the Internet delivers mail from one computer to another.

SMUT—See Simple Mail Transfer Protocol.

Software—The programs that are run on a computer system.

SSL—See Secure Sockets Layer.

Streaming—The process of receiving data continuously (typically sound or video) from a CD or the Internet, that eliminates the need for waiting to load the program before viewing.

Supply Chain Management—The system for efficient purchase and delivery of materials required in the process of manufacturing or operations, where timely delivery of the materials is critical.

T1—A communications standard, wide pipe that carries 24-voice calls or data 1.4 million BPS over a pair of telephone lines.

TCP/IP—A protocol, the system networks use to communicate with each other on the Internet.

Transaction—The record of exchanged goods and services. In E-Commerce, it is the process of a payment request, including merchant account, consumer's credit card details and payment amount referred to an acquiring bank for approval or rejection.

Uniform Resource Locator (URL)—This is the unique web address used in a web browser, for example, www.AppallasoPublishing.com.

Universal Serial Bus (USB)—A serial interface or socket, standard on many computers, for adding peripheral devices such as game controllers, serial and parallel ports, and input devices.

UNIX—An operating system developed by AT&T.

URL—See Uniform Resource Locator.

USB—See Universal Serial Bus.

Uuencode/Uudecode–Programs that encode files to make them suitable for sending as e-mail. When the message arrives, the recipient can run uudecode to turn it back into the original file.

Virtual Organization—An organization that is not dependent on the physical location of offices or buildings, but rather through 24/7 global connectivity, portability and flexibility, networks people and things around the world to achieve valuable exchange relationships that serve the organization with little if any need for tangible infrastructure.

Virtual Reality—A 3D simulation that replicates actual real-time experiences.

VRML—A language used for building virtual reality pages.

WAP—See Wireless Application Protocol.

WAV (.wav File)—A popular format for sound files found on the Internet.

Wireless Application Protocol (WAP)—An adaptation of HTTP to support mobile devices such as cell or mobile phones. Used in North America primarily as a bridge between 2G and 3G wireless web.

Wireless Markup Language (WML)—One of a series of adaptations of HTML. Language designed to bridge 2G and wired web access into the wireless world; allows specially designed Web pages to be presented on certain mobile phones and personal digital assistants via wireless access.

WML—See Wireless Markup Language.

XHTML—See Extensible Hypertext Markup Language.

XML—See Extensible Markup Language.

ZIP (.zip File)—A compressed file that helps reduce file sizes, especially for transferring or downloading through the Internet.

NOTES

Introduction

1. My access to Wendy's International and the invaluable experiences of building and operating Wendy's franchise stores was not a product of astute planning or career design on my part. I had graduated from Arizona State University with a B.S. in Aerospace Engineering and a Flight Instructor's shingle with no idea what I wanted to be when I grew up. In their compassion, my Dad and cousin invited me to tag along as they began their Wendy's franchises in the Midwest. In short order we had all been through Wendy's Operators school in Dublin, Ohio, (which was seminal laying the foundation for many of the principles described herein), and had worked behind the counter in over a dozen of the first stores between Columbus and Kansas City.

Chapter 1-Limit Your Menu

1. In early 2000, WebCriteria gave useability ratings to some of the Internet's most popular sites—Hospitality and Travel. The conclusion? "In order to be successful,...sites must be easy to navigate, keep[ing] graphics compressed and their size to a minimum." "NUA Internet Surveys," *ZDNet*, May 22, 2000, <zdnet.com>.

2. In the business to business E-Commerce Report entitled, "The Secrets of Their Success—Profiles of Business to Business E-Commerce Leaders," IDC studied dozens of leading online enterprises; from American Express to Cisco and UPS. Two of the top recommendations: "fast navigation and relevant content." IDC, February 14, 2000, <www.idc.com>.

3. According to a series of joint studies in online retail by Bain & Company and Mainspring, the more often a customer visits a site, the more likely that customer will spend an increasing amount of money and generate more profits for the online retailer. For example, in apparel, the average repeat customer spent 67 percent more overall in the third year of his or her shopping relationship with an online retail vendor than in the first six months. And, over three years, customers referred by online grocery shoppers spent an additional 75 percent of what the original shop spent. The study surveyed Web shoppers within industry sectors including apparel, groceries, and electronics. Given the high cost of acquiring customers, the results show that for e-tailers to recoup that investment, they need to convince customers to return to their site again

and again. The study found that the average online apparel shopper was not profitable for the retailer until he or she had shopped at the site four times. This implies that the retailer has to retain the customer for 12 months in order to break even. Darrell Rigby, "Panning for Gold: The Power of Customer Segmentation in Online Retailing," *eStrategy Brief*, May 31, 2000, <bain.com>.

Chapter 2-Keep the Numbers in Focus

1. The Greek word euangelistes, translated to the English word evangelist, means "a messenger of good." I intend no disrespect to those ambassadors who bring the ultimate good news—the Gospel message, but only infer a loose association that many still need to hear the news about E-Business.

2. All the stories and cases described in these chapters and throughout this work are real. In many cases, like this one, individual's names have been disguised as a courtesy; but to almost every other detail including company sizes, industries and situations, I've endeavored to accurately and candidly reflect the scenarios and dialogues as they happened.

3. In a survey of more than 1000 U.S. workers, of those using a computer at work, the great majority (87%) said they use it for job-related activities, with e-mail, word processing, browsing the Net, and gathering news and information leading the list of applications. Less than 16% indicated that they sometimes use it for personal interests. Gene Koretz, "Workers Want a High Tech Edge," *Business Week*, February 28, 2000, <businessweek.com>.

Chapter 3-Let Customers in On Your Secrets

1. Direct Marketing Association's Marketing to Business Conference, Keynote Speech, Orlando, Florida, February, 1999.

2. Some have held out for old-style secret-keeping longer than others. It wasn't until early 1999 that Merrill Lynch finally bit the bullet, and slowly began to offer online trading, albeit in an exclusive "club" sort of way. As a Merrill Lynch customer in April of 1999, you could move to online trading as long as you didn't mind paying between $43 to over $90 per trade. The commission charged was based on a complex formula that almost guaranteed that no one would pay the same fees as the next person. Contrast that with the simple, straightforward approach that the other online brokers took, and its obvious why so many captured marketshare early.

Chapter 4-Fast or Not at All

1. As the number of Internet users increases, so does the desire for a faster connection, according to a survey conducted by research firm The Yankee Group. Forty-one percent of Net surfers were very interested in high-speed Internet access and an additional forty-three percent were somewhat interested. The survey also found that users are more willing to pay more for the high-speed data connections. Thirty-six percent of online households are willing to pay $40 per month—the typical price for

cable modem service—for high-speed access, up from twenty-seven percent. Cable and telephone companies are only beginning to offer fast access. The Yankee Group estimates that about 300,000 subscribers can now receive high-speed Internet service, with telephone companies servicing fewer subscribers with Digital Subscriber Line service.

The fast Internet market is slated to boom in the next few years. The Yankee Group predicted that households subscribing to high-speed access will grow from fewer than 500,000 in 1999 to 7 million in 2002. "High Speed Market Set to Explode," January 28, 2000, <Internettelephony.com>.

2. Recognize that this predisposition to speed and expectation for things to move fast is not limited to the confines of your E-Business system alone. Everything about business happens at a rate and pace today that would have been unthinkable a few short years ago. As guru Gary Hamel sees it: "It's not only product life-cycles that are shrinking; strategy cycles are shrinking. Companies are going to have to reinvent themselves much more frequently than before." Gary Hamel, "Today's Companies Won't Make It, and Gary Hamel Knows Why," *Fortune Magazine*, September 4, 2000, page 386.

3. Purchasing Magazine, February 11, 1999, <www.manufacturing.net/magazine/purchasing>.

4. Gauge the speed of the Web with the latest data from Keynote Systems' Business 40 Index, a monitor of download times at 40 major business websites. Average download time of a homepage for a business connection was 6 seconds in mid 1999, 4.4 seconds in mid 2000. "Internet Economy Indicators," *The Industry Standard,* June 22, 2000, <www.thestandard.com>.

Chapter 5-Keep Your Core Operations Intact

1. One of the early high flyers that forgot this was PlanetRx, who thought that selling shampoo and aspirin on the Net was a formula for success. Unfortunately for them, because corner drug stores are everywhere, Net sales don't offer much more convenience, and most grocery shoppers pick up these items while shopping for food. For 1999, this ill-fated idea cost them almost $4 for every $1 they sold. Company sales were hamstrung at around $9 million per quarter in 2000, on which it lost more than $35 million per quarter. "There was an amount of hubris in thinking that they could radically shift the way consumers have always purchased health and beauty aids," says Claudine Singer, a market researcher at Jupiter Communications, Inc." Claudine Singer, "Drug Doldrums," *Business Week E-Biz*, July 24, 2000, <businessweek.com>.

2. As Business Week reported, in the heady days of dot com mania, Value America's founder Craig Winn pitched the idea of a company without inventory as a strength, modeled after the Price Club or Costco warehouse concept where buying in quantity meant savings by cutting out the middleman. In August 2000 when Value America announced it was filing for Chapter 11, The Industry Standard recapped the demise. When first launched, they reported, Value America "...could be nimble and efficient because it wouldn't be saddled with overhead...[But] things grew too fast. Soon, Value America's product lines had mushroomed to

include everything from computers to cheesecake to barbecued spareribs...but many of Value America's vendors weren't geared up to ship just one computer or cheesecake, and naturally gave individual orders a low priority." August 11, [2000] shared were trading at 70 cents, down from $74 in April, 1999." Keith Perine, "An American Dream Gone Bad," *The Industry Standard*, August 28, 2000, page 71.

3. There *are* rare exceptions to this rule. Egghead is one of the few businesses in the 1990's that was able to radically transform their business operating model from retail only to online only, and survive. With one stroke of the virtual pen, the company decided to close eighty physical retail stores, and announced they were going to be called Egghead.com from then on. Purists would argue that Egghead's story demonstrates that core business operations can be abandoned successfully in the Connected Economy, and that all retailers could have the same result as Egghead.com. While I do think there may be some cases where Egghead's story could be replicated with equal success, I would also counter that most retail establishments do not offer products that have become commodities like Egghead's had. Going into a mall to find an Egghead retailer to buy a software program in a box was already a losing proposition long before Egghead decided to shutter stores. Software was available everywhere, from the endless stream of catalogs that came in the mail almost daily, to the manufacturer, to the new online marketplaces. Even if the Egghead store staff did offer extra value like customer service, the consumer didn't value it as such. So converting to online was really Egghead's only choice. On the other hand, buying a pair of pants in a retail store is quite different than buying that pair or pants online, and customers have shown that for products that are not commodities, where touching and feeling is encouraged, the physical store still has a place.

4. Even one of the early adopters of online service, the banking industry, fell victim to this trap. According to eMarketer's newly released eBanking Report, despite the rally cries of E-Commerce analysts, online banking has yet to live up to its expectations. For at least 18 months, the banking industry has been told by almost every newspaper or magazine article written on the topic that traditional retail banking faced impending doom at the hands of online banks. It didn't turn out that way.

Since their establishment, pure Internet banks had only accounted for 0.02% of $9.6 billion found in FDIC insured deposits by year end 1999. Of the 18 billion billing transactions, only 4.2 million were handled online. Since then, the numbers have risen, but few buildings have been closed in favor of online banking.

Why? According to the report, banks "mistakenly followed the advice of E-Commerce analysts too closely and disregarded their own intuition when developing their creative strategies, namely online banking. In particular, the eBanking Report notes four false premises: 1) Retail banking is the same as retail commerce; 2) Since online retail trading succeeded, online banking will succeed also; 3) Internet banking is convenient; 4) The affluence of Internet users equals profitability for Internet banks."

"Too many analysts began from false propositions when they argued why online banking would succeed," states Paul Mulligan, author of the eBanking Report. "Obviously, when you begin a business plan from an invalid premise, you're guaranteed disjunctive results."
Paul Mulligan, "eMarketer's eBanking Report Reveals Short-Comings in Online Banking," *eMarketer*, June 21, 2000, <emarketer.com>.

Chapter 6-Fix Mistakes Unequivocally

1.   Jim Collins, "Best Beats First," *Inc. Magazine*, August, 2000, page 46.

2.   For more on your E-Business culture with regard to mistakes, see the article "How to Create an E-Culture" appearing in E-Business Advisor Magazine, September 2000, page16-23. Jessica Keyes, *Handbook of E-Business*, (Warren, Gorham and Lamont, 2000).

Chapter 7-Show More Than Tell

1.   While this may sound somewhat like a contradiction to the principle of delivering your site content "Fast or Not at All" as discussed in Chapter 4, (because images and graphics so often take longer to load than HTML text), it does not necessarily have to be that way. Yahoo!'s financial sites as mentioned previously are legend for their lack of graphics and images on the homepages, and those sites are among the fastest loading in the industry. But the moment you go to any stock or investment screen, the first thing you see is a chart showing performance. And the majority of information you find by clicking through that stock's page is delivered in chart or graph form. There are a variety of other ways to "show" your information besides using images. For more information on how different elements on a page affect load speeds, there are articles on the ZDNet.com system, and programs such as Dreamweaver by Macromedia that allow you to "test" elements and see resultant tables of various load times on different platforms.

2.   This quote was attributed to Rafe Needleman, editor of Red Herring Online, at the "Muddy" awards ceremony. Matthew Boersma, "Muddies Unveil Terrible Beauties," *ZDNet News*, May 7, 1999, <zdnet.com>.

Chapter 8-Give Free Refills

1.   In a candid interview with Jim Evans, Steven Brill exposed the basic flaws behind APB News and Salon's inability to convince users that they should pay them for their content, when the rest of the online universe was free. It was an enlightening piece. Steven Brill, "Information wants to Be Free—That's the Problem," *The Industry Standard*, June 19, 2000, <thestandard.com>.

2.   As AOL discovered when they converted their pricing model from usage fees (where you paid more the longer you were on) to flat rates like other ISPs, when community is free, growth happens.

3.   Roger C. Parker, *Relationship Marketing on the Internet*, (Holbrook, Adams Media Corporation, 2000).

Chapter 9-Leverage Your Ingredients

1. For a Flash producer in your area, go to the Macromedia site at http://www.macromedia.com and search under developers or partners.

Chapter 10-Give Customers the Order Pad

1. Lauren Barack's treatment of this phenomenon in Business 2.0 is worth checking out. She puts it this way: "Like it or not, there is a fundamental power shift taking place in the online marketing world. Consumers are learning that they hold the power to choose what they want to see, when, and how often." Lauren Barack, "Pretty, Pretty, Please," *Business 2.0*, April, 2000,<Business2.0.com>.

2. Charles Pappas, "What is an Extranet?" <ZDNet.com>.

3. As far back as September, 1999, customer Extranets were ranked in the Top Ten of E-Business tools. "Implementing Next-generation E-Business Strategies," ActiveMedia, September 1999, <Active-Media.com>.

4. Surfers expect personal treatment from online firms. Cyber Dialogue found 88 percent of U.S. Internet users believe supplying a site with personal information is the best way for companies to know their customers. CyberDialogue "re:Source," December 1999, <Internet-User.com>.

Chapter 11-Know Your Customers by Name

1. Karen Solomon, "Customer Disservice 2000," *The Industry Standard*, July 24, 2000, <www.thestandard.com>.

2. In the critically acclaimed cover story entitled "The 21st Century Corporation," Business Week described this as no longer an option. "The era of mass production, mass marketing, and even mass media is over. Customers will be calling the shots from how on." Wendy Zellner, "Hey, Are You Listening to Me?" *Business Week*, August 28, 2000, page 138.

3. Chad Kaydo, "As Good As It Gets," *Sales and Marketing Management*, March, 2000, page 55.

4. FloNetwork, an online direct marketing application service provider, in connection with NFO Interactive found a strong and positive response for opt-in e-mail marketing in a recent survey. The survey of 1,000 net users found that 94% of consumers opt-in for permission based e-mail. Fully 89% of those surveyed think that e-mail is a good way to get information about products of interest to them. Among consumers with existing relationship with merchants, 81% think that e-mail is a good way to communicate with them. The survey also confirms that consumers will trade personal information for services. Given a clear privacy policy, 54% of respondents said they would part with information in exchange for personalized service. This compares to 22% that won't and 23% who are neutral on the issue. EMarketer, Flo Network/NFO Interactive Survey, July 1, 2000, <emarketer.com>.

5. Lauren Barack, "Pretty, Pretty Please," *Business 2.0*, April, 2000, page 176.

6. "Permission E-mail: The future of Direct Marketing," ITM Strategies, found in "Permission to Succeed," *Los Angeles Business Journal, January 31, 2000*, <labusinessjournal.com>.

7. It is reported that over three quarters of all Internet users access e-mail at least daily. Jupiter Communications, December 1999, <jup.com>.

8. Peppers & Rogers Group, "1 to 1 E-mail," *1 to 1 Magazine*, May, 2000, page 8ff.

9. Peppers & Rogers Group, 8ff.

10. Peppers & Rogers Group, 8ff.

11. Response rates of 8% or more for e-mail campaigns targeting opt-in users are not only common, but they've become relatively easy to attain. At Brighton One-to-One, Donna Cooper has seen campaigns with response rates of over 40%. In late summer of 2000, she directed an e-mail project for one of North America's largest banks that pulled a 12% response rate...on the first day!

Chapter 12-Using and Managing Outside Vendors

1. John Ellis, "Digital Matters," *Fast Company*, April, 2000, page 336.

2. John Ellis, page 336.

3. John Ellis, page 336.

4. Lewis Pinault, *Consulting Demons: Inside the Unscrupulous World of Global Corporate Consulting*, (New York, Harper Business, 2000) page 43ff.

5. Lewis Pinault, page 43ff.

6. In November, 1999, W.L. Gore & Associates slapped Deloitte & Touche and its Deloitte Consulting arm with a suit, alleging the firm botched the setup of a new human-resources program designed by PeopleSoft, Inc. Gore, the makers of Gore-Tex brand fabrics, claimed that, after convincing company execs of it expertise with PeopleSoft systems, Deloitte's consultants usually appeared flummoxed about how to proceed. "They were always on the phone with PeopleSoft, asking them what to do next," says Jay W. Eisenhofer, an attorney representing Gore. Dean Foust, "First Sue All Consultants," *Business Week*, July 17, 2000, page 96.

7. Mark Mehler, ZDNet Opinion, Citing Giga Information Group Research, March 31, 2000, <zdnet.com>.

8. Mark Mehler, <zdnet.com>.

9. *Fast Company*, May, 2000, <www.fastcompany.com>.

10. Jane Hodges, "Divide and Conquer," *Business 2.0*, April, 2000, page 155.

11. Worldwide Partners agencies are in over 60 major cities around the world, and through connectivity offer a virtual smorgasbord of the best services from the best specialists in the industry. For organizations looking for an easy way to survey scores of firms, or those looking for strength in markets around the world, a single inquiry at http://www.wwpartners.com will generate a bevy of options and a number of potential agency resources to choose from.

12. *AAAA Program Guide*, May, 2000, <www.AAAA.org>.

13. Dean Gooderham Acheson, US Secretary of State, (1893-1971).

14. Transforming an ad agency into an E-centric organization for the Connected Economy involves a lot more than simply promoting the

in-house IT manager to a new E-Business title or role. Those agencies that are doing so for real will have embraced the concept philosophically, and committed to it financially. When Roger Yount of the Brighton Agency first started envisioning the transformation of his agency for the New Economy, he backed his vision with a long-term commitment, and the company checkbook. With buy-in from Controller Sandy Coons, and full support from other founding partners Drew Fitzgerald and Kevin Monahan, over a period of about three years Roger purchased companies, hired key experts, and invested in the infrastructure necessary to truly be what everyone else was only talking about. Long before "one-to-one" and "permission marketing" was hot, Brighton had purchased The Alan Company in St. Louis, one of the two top direct-on demand-printers in the city, and a warehouse fulfillment center downtown. He tapped John Kruszka from Xerox to direct the printing operation and hired Donna Cooper to head up the Brighton Direct side. He brought William "Chip" Schafer in as new C.O.O. to help manage the new enterprises as a collective whole, and moved Activated Multimedia, Inc.'s entire staff and operations into Brighton's building in Clayton, including servers, T-1s, and Sega Dreamcast. With the addition of Steve Puckett as Creative Director and Ted Haller in media, by the time the Brighton Agency sign came down (literally) in January 2000, and BrightonUSA was officially born, the word "agency" was practically and obviously no longer applicable to the organization Brighton had become. Today, BrightonUSA rarely has a client or project that does not have some aspect of E-Business woven into the mix.

15. "Net Prophet," *Webcentric*, March, 2000, <webcentricman.com>.

16. Scott Kirsner, "Collision Course," *Fast Company*, January, 2000, <www.fastcompany.com>.

17. On March 1, 2000, USWeb/CKS inked another merger deal, this time with supply-chain management specialists Whittman-Hart, making it a $14 billion company. Wisely, the new conglomerate did not add another slash or hyphen to an already cumbersome moniker, and instead chose the more compact "March First."

18. Eryn Brown, "E-Consultants," *Fortune Magazine*, April 12, 1999, <www.fortune.com>.

19. Eryn Brown, <www.fortune.com>.

20. Michael Simon, "Going Public: What a Difference a Year Makes," *Red Herring*, May, 2000, pages 38-40.

21. The business Carnegie built out of a newly discovered technology over a century ago is worth noting today. At the locus of another tectonic shift in business, the Industrial Revolution of the 1800's, the modern world was forever changed when molten pig iron was forced through a Bessemer converter to form a new stronger and more refined metal called steel. That it was harder and more resilient than any other material at the time was only part of the story...that it could be molded and shaped in the process was even more important. For in the shaping of steel comes the real benefit of steel— now any business could use it to improve their own products and services, and increase value while doing so. Carnegie's secret wasn't in knowing *how* the technology worked, it was in recognizing what it could do. Because he could see end-results

and envision (ex-nihilo) products at the end of that molten trough, he enabled the rails, engines, bridges and thousands of other innovations to be birthed.

22. Carlye Adler, "Going Online? Don't Sacrifice Marketing for Technology," *Fortune Magazine,* October 25, 1999, <www.fortune.com>.

23. Elizabeth Millard, "Instant Intellect," *Business 2.0,* December 1999, <www.business2.0.com>.

24. Cohan breaks the project down into six phases: 1) Identifying the capabilities needed; 2) Analyzing your organization's capability gaps; 3) Hiring an outside consultant, if necessary; 4) Anticipating the effort of integration; 5) Fixing the time and cost of the development process; and 6) Being prepared to modify the system after launch. Peter S. Cohan, *eProfit,* (New York, Amacom, 2000), page 130.

Chapter 13-Do it Yourself with ASP "Apps on Tap"

1. Fred Sandsmark, "High Hurdles for Small Business," *Red Herring,* March, 2000, <www.redherring.com>.

2. Fred Sandsmark, <www.redherring.com>.

3. Matt Carmichael, "NetB2B," *Web Price Index,* May 22, 2000, <netB2B.com>.

4. Erica Garcia, "The Web Store Solution," *Money Magazine,* September 2000, page 147.

5. Stewart McKie, "Outsourcing with ASPs in the Internet Age," *Business Finance Magazine,* November, 1999, page 61.

6. Additional highlights from the survey: Slightly more than half–52 percent–of respondents who qualified for the survey (either using an ASP or planning to in the next year) said their companies are currently accessing applications on a "rental" or "as needed" basis through an application service provider or application hosting organization. Of the 48 percent who aren't, all said their companies plan to access computer applications in that fashion sometime within the next 12 months.

Most respondents who are using an ASP model indicated that they are currently purchasing between two and six applications from an ASP. That number is consistent with what these business executives expect to access through the ASP model over the next year.

The most important factors in influencing the ASP purchase decision were a reduction in the total cost of application ownership; the ability to focus on achieving strategic business objectives; and the freeing of IT resources to focus on internal mission critical applications.

Zona Research, Inc., of Redwood City, California, June 1, 2000, <ASPIndustry.org>.

7. Here's how Fortune Magazine described it in late 1999: "It's now possible to set-up a Web page and conduct electronic commerce in a matter of minutes, with no up-front costs. No longer must you learn the intricacies of HTML and JavaScript, master Web-design software, or hire someone to build your site. Companies such as Bigstep.com, eCongo and freemerchant.com have packaged all the basic tools and made them available for free. Using only a browser, you can choose a Website template suited to your specific type of business—housewares,

consulting, or sports equipment, say. Write the descriptive text, add images of the products you want to sell, and within minutes your site is up on the Web and accessible to millions." "Build Your Own E-Business," *Fortune Magazine*, December 1, 1999, <library.northernlight.com>.

8.   G. Beato, "Web-o-Matic," *Business 2.0*, October, 1999, pages 193-197, <www.business2.0.com>.

9.   Monua Janah, "Aspiring to Serve," *Red Herring*, June, 2000.

10. Trever Gruen-Kennedy, ASPIC, *ASPNews Online*, 2000, <aspnews.com>.

11. Ronna Abramson and Eric Young, "Fedex Courts Small Business," *The Industry Standard*, June 26, 2000, <thestandard.com>.

12. "Intel Joins the Party," *ASPNews*, July 10, 2000, <aspnews.com>.

13. Author, <aspnews.com>.

14. Site builders, Store builders and E-Commerce are only a small fraction of the categories that are available to organizations, offering the same easy to use, rent as you go arrangement. Today there online pay as you go resources that also cover:

·   Customer Relationship Management (CRM)
·   Desktop apps
·   E-Business
·   Enterprise Resource Planning (ERP)
·   Financials
·   Human Resources (HR)
·   Info sharing and management
·   Manufacturing
·   Vertical Markets

In short, if there has been a solution or program out there in a software package, you can almost guarantee that you can find it now on the Internet, in an ASP framework. For more exhaustive information about the broader scope of ASP solutions, go to ASPNews.org.

Chapter 14-ASP Reviews and Ratings

1.   Bridget Eklund, "E-Sourcing: Now Accepting Applications," *Red Herring*, September 2000, page 454, <www.redherring.com>.

INDEX

ABOUT THE AUTHOR

Not many can say their E-Business experience predates Amazon.com, but G. Liam Thompson has been bringing value-based digital tools and E-solutions to small businesses and Fortune 500 clients like Bausch & Lomb, May Company, BASF, Mallinckrodt, Monsanto, and Rubbermaid-Little Tikes since 1992. After moving to St. Louis from Los Angeles, Thompson and co-founder David Goldstein birthed one of the first E-Business-developing teams in the country, Activated Multimedia Inc. Based on their philosophy of "West Coast creativity with Midwestern values" and a willingness to try the newest ideas that most were only reading about, these early pioneers found dozens of early-adopting corporations entrusting their E-development to "the guys at the Barn."

In December 1997, G. Liam was awarded and named by his peers as one of the "Top 100" multimedia producers in the world. By 1998, Thompson had already personally managed the development of over 50 E-Business projects, invented over a dozen E-Business tools and products, and won a variety of industry awards. In 1998, as co-founder and President of Activated Training, LLC, he launched one of the first working ASP-based online training systems, TrainingDepartment.com, which today has over 1,500 corporate clients. In addition to serving as E-Business strategist for some of North America's leading B2B organizations, Thompson has launched three of his own E-Businesses and also directs Brighton Interactive, LLC, now one of the largest E-Business developers in the Midwest. He also serves as Vice President of BrightonUSA, St. Louis' largest connected communications company.

G. Liam is a graduate of the Webster University Business School, having earned a Masters in Marketing. He did his undergraduate work at Arizona State University, where he received a Bachelor of Science in Aerospace Engineering, as well as a Certified Flight Instructor rating. A popular speaker and lecturer at a number of colleges and campuses worldwide, Mr. Thompson has also written or edited over a dozen online titles, including *The Techies Guide to Interpersonal Skills*, *The Connected Manager's Guide to Stress Management*, and *Interactive Selling in the Connected Age*. A commercial and aerobatics pilot, Liam also supports the CBMC, YWAM, Mercy Ships, and inner city ministries. He lives in St. Louis County with wife, Lisa, and daughter, Tali, who keep his old scrapbook showing him building Wendy's franchise stores from '77-'79.

ABOUT APPALLASO

Appallaso – v. from *apo*, away or from; and *allaso*, to change, heal, or cure.

No, we're not named after a breed of horse, (that's Appaloosa), nor a pedigree dog (that's Lhasa Apso). Appallaso literally means "to change from" or "to transform" in Greek, and it is both our mission, as well as our mandate. We exist to provide books and other resources that help individuals and organizations change and improve in the new global marketplace.

Appallaso Publishing was created to serve the growing ranks of small business owners, managers and entrepreneurs looking for tools and resources to compete in the Connected Economy. Appallaso Publishing Group was birthed in the new economy, specifically *for* the new economy, so the old rules that governed traditional publishing do not apply. Unlike other presses that are economically bound to produce books in large quantities in order to offset the overhead and fixed costs inherited from the 20th century, Appallaso Publishing was created for the 21st-century, and can produce every title and resource in incremental quantities and in a variety of languages on demand. As markets open and grow in other connected regions of the globe, Appallaso is equipped to deliver at a speed commensurate with the Internet.

May We Hear From You?

Tell us What You Think

E-Business To Go and Appallaso Publishing Group are committed to providing the Small and Medium Business owner and operator the same depth of seminal, practical resources for competing and winning in the Connected Economy that big business enjoys, without the inflated cost or complexity. If you have a comment or suggestion, please let us know. We value your input! The feedback you provide helps us select new products and book topics, as well as improve existing books in future editions. Send your comments to: AppallasoDirector@hotmail.com.

Join the EB2GO Research Team

If you've discovered a tool, technology, or App on Tap that you think should be included in the next edition of EB2GO, or would like to join the EB2GO Research Team and participate in evaluating the same, we'd like to hear from you. Send your request along with your full name, address, phone number, fax number, and e-mail address to gLiam@E-BusinessToGo.com.

Sign up for Updates

If you'd like to be sent e-mail updates about new tools and technologies in the industry, new EB2GO publications and resources, or insights from the field and our EB2GO researchers, simply ask to be added to the e-mail list. Send your e-mail address to Updates@E-BusinessToGo.com.

Or, send any of the above by snail mail to:
Appallaso Publishing Group
P.O. Box 3985
St. Louis, Missouri, USA
63022-3985

Order Form

E-BUSINESS
TO GO

INSIDER SECRETS
TO MAKE YOUR SMALL BUSINESS
A **BIG** BUSINESS ON THE INTERNET

by G. LIAM THOMPSON

...is distributed in North America, Europe, Africa,
South America, and the Pacific Rim by leading wholesalers and
distributors to the trade. Ask for it at your local bookstore,
warehouse club, catalog or online retailer.
If you would like special autographed copies in quantity
use the form below.

Give autographed copies to everyone on your team:

Quantity	Price Each	Shipping Each	Total Each
5-10	$11.95	$3.00	$14.95
11-20	$10.95	$3.00	$13.95
21-50	$ 9.95	$3.00	$12.95
51-100	$ 8.95	$2.00	$10.95

—FOR A LIMITED TIME ONLY—

YES, I want _____ autographed copies of **E-Business To Go** at
$_____ each, plus $_____each for shipping for a subtotal of
$_____ each. My total price for _____ books therefore is $_____.

Check Enclosed   Check number: _____
Credit Card (circle one):   Visa   Amex   Mastercard
Card number:_____Expires:_____
Your Name:_____Organization:_____
Shipping Address:_____
City_____State:_____
Zip:_____Country:_____
Phone:_____ E-mail: _____

Please make checks payable to and send to:
Appallaso Publishing Group, PO Box 3985, St. Louis, MO 63022
Or e-mail to: AppallasoEditor@hotmail.com
Or fax to: 636-394-2216